GREAT
SCRAPBOOKS

▲ *HUGS, LOVE, AND KISSES, by Kristi Hazelrigg, Seminole, OK.*

MEMORY MAKERS®

GREAT SCRAPBOOKS

Ideas, Tips & Techniques

MICHELE GERBRANDT AND
JUDITH DURANT

BEAUX ARTS EDITIONS
IN ASSOCIATION WITH F&W PUBLICATIONS, INC.

© 2000 Hugh Lauter Levin Associates, Inc.
http://www.HLLA.com
ISBN: 0-88363-662-X

Project Director: Leslie Conron Carola
Design: Kathleen Herlihy-Paoli
Editor: Leslie Conron Carola
Copy Editor: Deborah Teipel Zindell

The page ideas featured are from the readers and artists of
Memory Makers ® scrapbook magazine, published by:
Satellite Press
C/O F & W Publications, Inc.
1507 Dana Avenue Avenue
Cincinnati, OH 45207
www.memorymakersmagazine.com

Idea Coordinator: Pennie Stutzman
Craft Coordinator: Pam Klassen
Photo Directors: Ron Gerbrandt and Linda Flemming
Photo Studios: Jim Cambon and Carol Conway
Photo Production: Diane Gibbs

This book is co-published by F & W Publications, Inc. and
Hugh Lauter Levin Associates, Inc.

Printed in China

CONTENTS

Mackenzie helping Aunt Vivie make brownies. She was a lot of help and had so much fun.

MILK

mackenzie 4 yr.

8/98

INTRODUCTION

What to do with a visiting niece on a late afternoon? Everybody loves brownies. Why not make a batch or two? And, in the process, make a friend for life. MacKenzie's mother took this brownie baking an enticing step forward by taking delightful photographs—and then creating a charming scrapbook page for MacKenzie to cherish forever. (Mother and aunt will cherish it as well.) And, who knows, we may have witnessed the first step in the development of a future pastry chef!

The ideas for creating a scrapbook can come from many sources. In this case, what to do on what might have been a boring afternoon became the driving force for an activity which a mother opted to preserve and remember—a child helping her aunt make brownies. No child could resist that offer, and no one could resist MacKenzie's 100-watt smile as she licks and stirs and licks! This is what childhood is all about. And this is just what scrapbooking is all about—savoring and then preserving life's moments—large and small, life-changing and life-affirming.

All families deserve to have their treasured memories kept alive, and certainly every family has more than enough stories to make an interesting book.

We all have stories to tell—simply by being alive. The stories are special because they are ours. And it is the collection of our stories that brings form and focus to our memories.

No wonder we love to scrapbook.

◀ MACKENZIE MAKES BROWNIES, by Veronica Gomes, Willows, CA. The images of MacKenzie, a baker at work, with brownie batter all over her hands and face will bring a smile to anyone's face for a long time. The simple page uses baking-theme stickers as decorative elements surrounding the bold single-theme photos of MacKenzie. The soft, rounded corners on the photos and mats and the homespun "stitched" lines add a nice touch. The written information completes the page with the date, MacKenzie's age, and the activity.

For centuries we have taken pleasure in the handwork of crafts. The instinct to create a book of memories is strong. And the pride that many women and men (yes, men *do* scrapbook) take in creating beautiful handmade objects for their homes is tremendous.

Much more than the sum of its parts, a great scrapbook page is a work of art. *Great Scrapbooks: Ideas, Tips & Techniques* offers the opportunity to learn the art of the craft from the best scrapbookers around the country—scrapbookers who take pride as well as pleasure in the pages they turn out for their families.

Many of our favorite pages have been created using special techniques. They are included here (at least one per chapter) with step-by-step process photos and easy-to-follow instructions. Lift-the-flaps, pop-ups, mosaics, pierced paper, punched paper, pieced paper, kaleidoscopes, die cuts, templates—you'll find them all here, with ideas on how and when to use them.

Keep treasured family memories alive. Dip into that box of old photos, or shoot some new pictures, and tell *your* family story in your own way.

▲ *Sweet Dreams, by Anna Walton, Barnhart, MO.*

Getting Organized

Rummaging through that old box of photos and reminiscing about the "good ol' days" is only the beginning of scrapbooking fun. But where do you start? The answer is, anywhere. You may simply choose a few photos and get right to it. But if you want to make sure you don't miss anything, start by organizing your photos.

Make a work area, gather a few essentials (a pen, stickie notes, etc.), decide on a type of album (either ongoing or specific), create categories and sort your photos within them. Be sure to store the photos in a safe environment.

Some may own castles on the banks of the Rhine,
And hire an orchestra each morning at nine,

But richer than I they will never be,
I have a daddy who spends time with me.

▲ *DADDY'S CASTLE, by Beth Ortstadt, Wichita, KS. Through the arched windows of a detailed reconstruction of a medieval castle we* *glimpse a father and child at play. Strong geometric shapes and a simple palette present the perfect backdrop for charming images.*

THE TOOLS

Albums come in a variety of shapes and styles, including post-bound, three-ring binder, and strap-style, all of which allow you to remove, add, or rearrange pages for ongoing projects. Spiral-bound albums are great for recording a special event or for gift giving. The quantity and size of your photos will help determine the size of the album you need. Make sure that the album you choose provides an acid-free, safe environment for your photos.

Decorative papers are available in a wide variety of eye-catching colors and patterns. Look for papers that are acid- and lignin-free to prevent fading or other damage to your photos. Papers are very versatile—use them to mat or frame photos, as an accent to your scrapbook page, or as a background for an entire page.

Use templates to shape paper or crop photos. Templates help you turn ordinary rectangular photos into whimsical shapes, cut decorative mats to enhance your photos, or create custom-made die cuts.

San Clemente, Ca.

March 1998

Playtime

at the

Park

What could be more fun than a brother that is a best friend!

Jake age 5

Jake & Cade on a spring day just made for fun!

Cade age 3

▲ *PLAYTIME AT THE PARK, by Pam Klassen, Denver, CO. Photographs by Elizabeth Wallis.*

Decorative scissors create unique edges on photos and papers. From elegant scallops to deckle-edged designs, there's a wide variety of patterns available. You'll also need a pair of sharp straight-edged scissors.

Look for glues, tapes, and mounting corners that are labeled "acid-free" and "photo-safe." Rubber cement, white glue, and cellophane tape contain chemicals that may adversely affect photos over time.

Journaling adds a voice as well as pertinent facts to a scrapbook. Journaling pens are available in a rainbow of colors, and a variety of pen tips makes fancy penmanship a breeze. Pigment ink pens are permanent, and your words won't fade like unrecorded memories.

STARTING A PROJECT

Armed with photos, album, and tools, you're ready to make your first page. Know what you want to accomplish and plan it out carefully before cropping any photos or affixing anything to the page.

1. CROPPING

Cropping your photos allows you to enhance the image by eliminating extraneous portions of the shot or by turning it into a unique shape. Create shaped photos by tracing around a template. Or create a silhouette by carefully cutting out the photo's subject and discarding the background. Before trimming, ask yourself if this portion of the photo adds interest, mood, or balance. Does it help date or place the subject? Taken out of context, can the image stand alone?

2. MATTING

Matting photos prior to mounting can help focus attention on the photos and add visual interest and balance to a page. Mat a cropped photo by adhering it to a piece of acid-free paper. Cover these with a template that is slightly larger than the photo. Trace around the template and cut. Or cut the mat freehand. For added dimension, make several layers of mats, each slightly larger than the previous one.

3. MOUNTING

It is not terribly tricky to mount photos in your album. Double-sided tapes and liquid adhesives create a permanent bond. Photo corners are paper or plastic triangles that are applied to the album page—photos are then slipped into the triangles. This allows you to place and easily remove photos from the album. Photo corners come in different sizes, shapes, and styles, from plain to fancy.

4. JOURNALING

Next to your photos, there is nothing more valuable than the information written about them. Who or what is that? Where are we? How long ago was this? These are the details that will disappear from memory over time if they aren't included in your scrapbook. Some subjective comments are also effective. What is being celebrated? What are your feelings about the event? Or place the event in a context. Each page has its own personality and its own reason for being part of your book.

Kaila, Alex, and Kylie had so much fun posing for these pictures in November 1998. Each of the girls received two of these pictures in frames as Christmas gifts. They were a big hit!

Kylie

Kaila

Alex

Best of

Friends

DESIGNING THE PAGE

Now that you know the basics, keeping these simple design ideas in mind will help you create scrapbook pages that are pleasing to the eye and the heart.

❖ *KEEP A FOCAL POINT.* The focal point is the primary image or area on the page—it's where the eye looks first. It may be a centrally located photo, a photo that is larger than the others on a page, a unique or exceptional photo, or a photo that is matted with a special paper or technique that makes it stand out from the others. Supporting images elaborate the main photo or theme. They may be smaller than the main photo and either depict the same scene or time as the primary shot or provide extra information.

❖ *CREATE BALANCE.* Large, bright, and busy photos feel heavier than their counterparts. Place your selected photos on the page and move them around until the page is balanced, that is, no one area overpowers the others. If you are creating a two-page spread, make sure the pages don't appear lopsided.

❖ *ADD COLOR.* Color sets mood, provides balance, and illuminates the photos on your page. Choose colors for background, mats, and accents that convey the feelings of the photos and the events they record. When it comes to color, less is sometimes more. Too much color can be a distraction.

With these basic techniques, there is no limit to the types and styles of scrapbook pages you can create. Remember to keep it simple when you start out; you don't have to fill the page with images.

◀ *BEST OF FRIENDS, by Tara Schneider, Virginia Beach, VA. Strong shapes dominate these cheerful pages. Photos are cropped, matted, and mounted in basic geometric shapes—the photos themselves dictated the cropped shape. The double matting (purple and then white) defines the images and draws the eye to the girls' happy faces. The photos can be cropped with commercial templates or with your own handmade templates once you've decided which parts of the photos you want to include on the scrapbook page.*

▶ *CHRISTMAS LIGHTS, by Joy Carey, Visalia, CA. Photos are matted with colored paper and cut with decorative-edged scissors. Using a light box, trace light bulbs onto white paper and color them with watercolors and black pen. Arrange and mount on the page as shown. Journal, label, and decorate the page with white pen.*

We presented three scrapbook artists with the same materials and instructions and waited to see the results. Each was given photos of Alexandra Nicole (photos by Erica Pierovich); three printed papers—floral, plaid, and squiggle; two colors of cardstock—yellow and blue. Instructions were minimal: Create a spring page using these photos, at least two of the papers, and any techniques and tools desired.

What better way to celebrate a spring day? Donna W. Pittard of Kingwood, Texas, created a coherent, dynamic design image (*opposite page*) that captures the essence of spring. Photos closely cropped in interesting shapes form a butterfly's outstretched wings, and the plaid paper is trimmed to mat the photos. The body of the butterfly was cut from cardstock and squiggle paper, and the antennae were created with circular journaling. Donna used an embossing stylus, decorating chalk, and cosmetic brushes (to apply the chalk) in addition to the materials provided.

Terri Robichon of Plymouth, Minnesota, cropped her photos to sizes and shapes that accentuate the subject (*below right*). She matted two of the photos with the squiggle paper and arranged all on the floral paper. Using a letter stencil, she created the page title using cardstock, then added journaling with a pen.

Joy Carey of Visalia, California, added watercolor flowers to her page (*below left*)—the line art is adapted from the book, *Eliza Jane Originals: Welcome the Seasons* by Marie Cole. Joy cut strips of plaid paper and applied them as borders. The photos and title are matted with the squiggle paper, and the photos are applied to the mats with photo corners. All decorative lettering was done by hand.

TIP: BASIC CROPPING

❖ *Let the images dictate the cropping.* What is important in the photo? Why are you including it here? Where do you want the eye to focus?

❖ *Shape adds interest to a page.* Don't feel limited by the shape of the original photo. Experiment. Different themes are supported by the shapes of the images as well as by the decorative details.

▲ ROLLIN' ROLLIN' ROLLIN', *by Eve Lowey, Huntington Beach, CA. A wonderful series of action photos was taken as baby Jared was* rolling over. *The first shot sets the tone. Silhouetted remaining shots are overlapped to give the feeling of motion.*

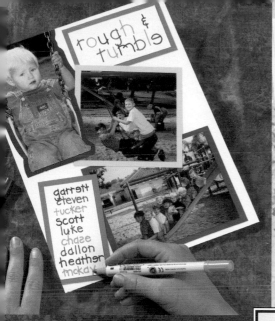

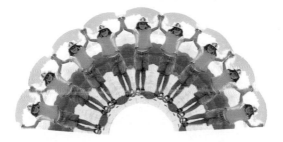

FAMILY

PAGES

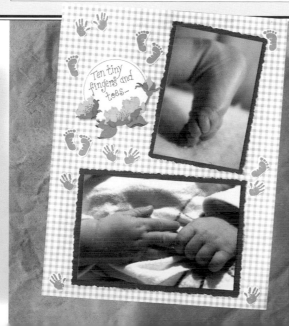

BABIES

Hands down, baby books are the most popular album themes at *Memory Makers* magazine. Requests for baby book scrapbook page ideas outnumber every other category by 4 to 1. Is it any wonder? How else can parents and grandparents and aunts and uncles celebrate this awe-inspiring event? There really is nothing that pulls a family closer together than the celebration of the birth of a child. What hope, what faith in the future, what trust! And all of it deserves to be celebrated and honored in the best way we know how. Creating a memory book to be cherished by generations of family members is an appropriate and loving celebration gift for the new being. Many people who may never have considered scrapbooking do so when a baby is born into their lives.

As with any scrapbook, a baby album requires both a plan and photos. One of the nicest aspects of scrapbooking is the opportunity it presents to include ideas and techniques from other crafts. Quilting has always been an important craft, and quilt patterns are a popular motif with scrapbookers. What you can do with fabric you can do with paper. Quilt patterns can be adapted to create beautiful frames, borders, or even the central motif on a large page. The quilt template used in the scrapbook page presented on the opposite page is a wonderful way to piece together a quilt pattern to set off the tender images of parents with their newborn infant. The quilt reminds us of tradition, of family; the photos speak solidly of warmth and love.

▶ *FLORAL QUILT, by Scarlett Clay, Leander, TX. This page, inspired by a magazine quilt pattern, is a clever and decorative way to use lots of pictures. To make a quilt pattern or template, photocopy and enlarge to the appropriate size the scrapbook page as shown on the facing page, or try drawing your own templates. Then use the templates to crop your photos. The flowers/leaf pieces, stems, and frames can be cut from patterned paper (as these were), or try painting some paper yourself before cutting it.*

Jacob's 1st Year

Cupid's Calendar

Each picture taken on the 14th of every month starting with February 14, 1995

The idea of photos in a context is of particular importance and probably most evident with baby pages. We observe the growth of a child in stages and compare these stages to other benchmarks—size, abilities, interests, etc. A year's worth of photos of Jacob (*shown opposite*) in the same chair with the same teddy bear on the same day of each month is a wonderful synthesis of growth in an infant's first year. "Cupid's Calendar"— Jacob was a Valentine's Day baby—is clever and perfectly appropriate.

Theme pages are a great way to use up extra or miscellaneous photos. Consider a "picture perfect" page that includes great photos not linked to other pages. A page that features your baby in different settings and times with a special toy is another possibility. Some scrapbookers use color to pull a layout together. Simply choose photos with a similar color scheme and use the color in the title for the page.

TIP: SAVE EVERYTHING!

Baby Memorabilia & Photo Checklist:
Shower invitations
Wrapping paper or ribbons
Photos of baby "equipment"
Ultrasound pictures
Bassinet name tag
Doctor's business card
Photo of hospital and nursery
Hospital and official birth certificates
Hospital bracelet
Handprints and footprints
Hospital bill
Birth announcement
Newspaper birth announcement
Cards from family and friends
Gift list and registry
Baby food, formula, and diaper labels
Growth and development records
Lock of hair
Small articles of clothing
Baby pictures of mom and dad

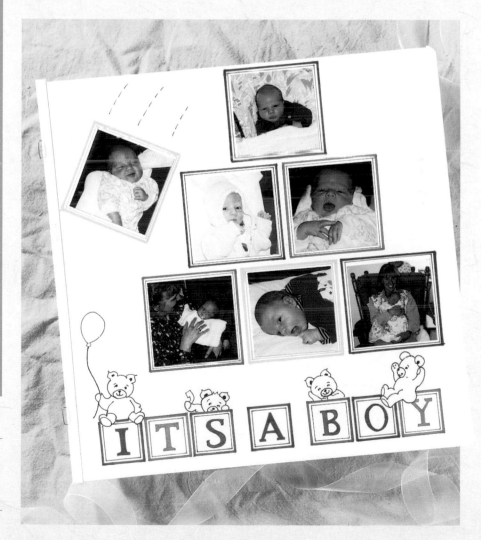

▶ *IT'S A BOY! by Karin Hrywko, Orlando, FL. A grandson's birth announcement functions as the design theme for the first page.*

◀ *JACOB'S 1ST YEAR, by Renee Belina, Apple Valley, MN.*

▲ BABY SHOWER, *by Yuko Neal, Huntington Beach, CA. A baby shower for a sister provides the inspiration for these pretty pages. Using different border designs of the same color for each page—there are ten in all—simultaneously unifies and highlights the acitivities of the party.*

it's not the end of the world

it's just intermission

APRIL 1998

▲ IT'S JUST INTERMISSION, *by Kim Bunton, Bloomington, IN. We can all relate to Kim's story. All she wanted was an angelic picture of Samantha in the dress given to her by her grandparents. But what she ended up with was a picture of Samantha in a different mood, furious at her mother for having put her in such an uncomfortable dress! The mats for the photo and journaling labels reiterate a dominant color in the background printed paper and serve to bring our focus to the less-than-happy infant dressed in her finest.*

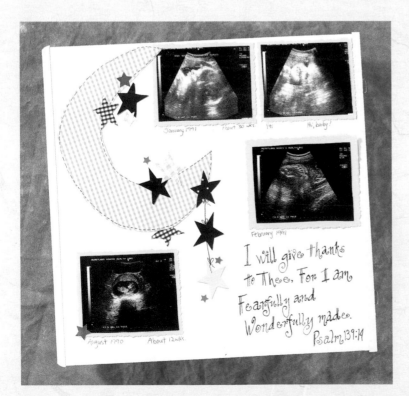

I will give thanks to Thee, For I am Fearfully and Wonderfully made. Psalm 139:14

◀ I WILL GIVE THANKS SONOGRAM, *by Kimberly Moore, Hutchinson, KS. First photos of your baby need not be taken after the baby's birth. With today's technology, we can have a record of every step along the way, in pictures that could certainly be the first in your baby's book.*

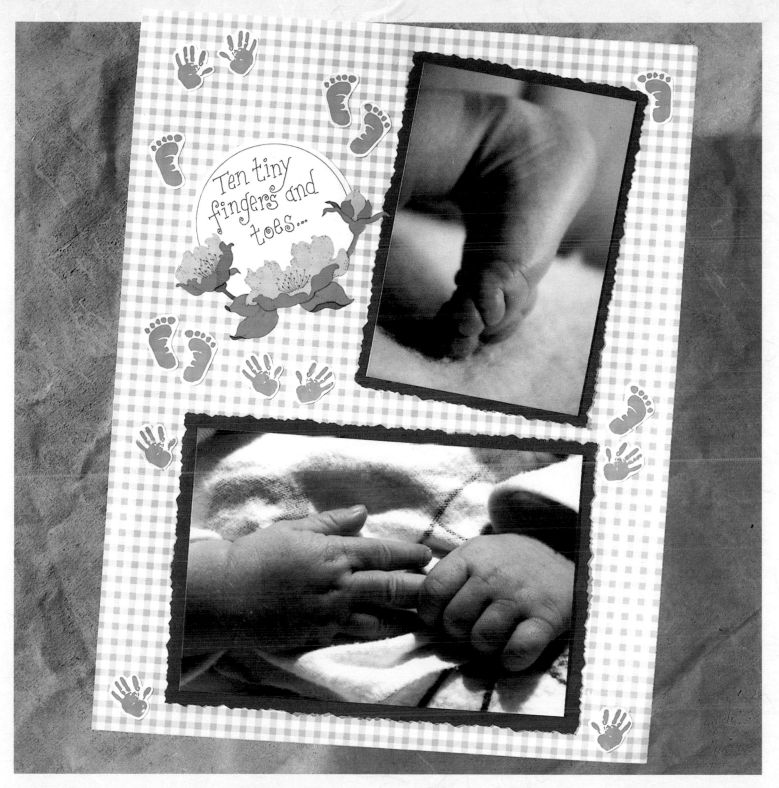

▲ TEN TINY FINGERS & TOES, *by Kristi Hazelrigg, Seminole, OK. Nothing typifies a new baby more than fingers and toes. How many times did we as new mothers count them? The simple black-and-white photos cradled in pink capture the dreamy mood.*

▶▶*(Overleaf)* CALEB'S BULLETIN BOARD, *by Kelly Clauss, Yorba Linda, CA. A charming bulletin board clearly reflects the goings-on in a typical home with active children. The informal placement of the photos and the decorative push pin art add a casual look to the page.*

o do list:
1. Kiss my mommy
2. play w/ daddy
3. sleep
4. eat
5. stroller ride
6.

MOMMY

PAPER PIERCING

Creative scrapbookers find inspiration almost anywhere. Paper piercing evolved from fifteenth-century parchment craft, which uses a number of techniques to create a design on parchment paper. Our basic example uses the techniques of embossing, cross-hatching, piercing, and perforating to yield an exquisite, lace-like design. To make the fancy heart frame, first photocopy and enlarge the heart design to the desired size. Use a dark pen to trace along the lines, making them easier to see. Then tape parchment paper over the pattern and trace with a white pencil or pen. Do not trace the cross-hatching. Now follow these steps:

STEP 1.

After tracing your design, place it right side down on an embossing pad, dense felt, or a computer mouse pad. Use an embossing tool (stylus) to trace along the white lines, applying enough pressure to change the parchment from gray to white. Fill in areas by gently rubbing the stylus from side to side, gradually increasing the pressure as the paper turns white.

STEP 2.

To cross-hatch, place your design right side down on an embossing pad. Use a ruler and a fine-tipped embossing stylus to emboss the grid lines. Press lightly so that the cross-hatches appear fainter than your embossed lines.

STEP 3.

To pierce, place your design on a thick felt pad. Using a piercing tool, pierce your design as desired. Pierce the parchment paper so that the colored paper you will eventually place under the parchment will show through the pierced spots. If you are piercing for decoration along a line, leave at least the width of one hole between each piercing.

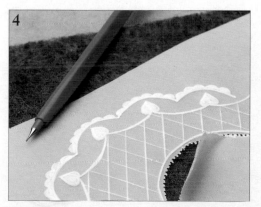

STEP 4.

To remove an outside edge or inside section, pierce just outside the embossed edges, placing the holes very close together (basically creating a perforated edge, ready for smooth tearing). To tear away the waste paper, press down near the perforated line and gently remove the waste paper.

SUPPLIES

* ❖ Parchment and colored papers
* ❖ Embossing pad and stylus
* ❖ Piercing tool
* ❖ White pencil or pen

CREATING A PUZZLE PAGE

This page uses the Coluzzle®—a sturdy plastic template that lets you crop photos into perfectly interlocking puzzle pieces. Coluzzles allow you to fit together several pictures into neat puzzle shapes, much like children's jigsaw puzzles. The templates are available in rectangle, star, heart, oval, teddy bear, and flowerpot shapes. These templates offer a completely new approach to cropping photos. This teddy bear Coluzzle (*shown opposite*) offers a whimsical way to combine five different photos in one 8 x 10-inch space.

See Sources (page 116) for the Coluzzle Scrapbooking Kit. Each kit includes a reusable template, a swivel knife designed specifically for the Coluzzle template channels, a straight knife for trimming, and a foam cutting mat (a regular self-healing mat will not work with the swivel knife).

1. GATHER PHOTOS AND PLAN LAYOUT

Collect photos and determine which to use for each puzzle piece. Use the template to make sure each photo fits the corresponding piece. To keep the focus on the page, subjects should face forward or toward the center of the layout.

2. CROP THE PHOTOS

For each puzzle piece, orient the photo as desired under the template. Place the photo and template on top of a foam cutting mat. Securely holding the template over the photo, place the tip of the swivel knife within each cutting channel and cut along each edge of the template.

3. TRIM PIECES AND ASSEMBLE

Remove the template and use a straight knife or scissors to make the final trims that connect each cutting line. Carefully remove the finished puzzle piece from the photo background. Assemble and arrange the design on your scrapbook page. A repositionable adhesive will allow you to move the pieces around before permanently bonding the design to your page. Embellish and journal as desired.

▶ *A BEARY SPECIAL GIRL, by Gail Means, Escondido, CA, and Marie Lariviere, Hanover, MA.*

▶ QUINN'S 2ND BIRTHDAY, *by Amy E. Carrell, Des Moines, IA. A giant freehand-cut numeral almost fills the page and certainly fills the bill. We know what to celebrate here. Silhouetted photos mounted strategically around the large "2" keep the birthday boy in focus. Decorative stickers embellish the colorful page.*

◀ HANDLE WITH CARE, *by Linda Rozolis, Cary, IL. Isn't it true? Kids have more fun with the packaging than what's in it! The large box was freehand cut and filled with matted photos.*

▼ FIRST DRAWING, *by Marsha Peacock, Jacksonville, FL. Here's the perfect time to let your children scribble right on the page. Thick colored pens and crayon stickers are all the supplies you need, in addition to the photos and a little art direction.*

◀ 15 MONTHS OLD, *by Ellen Underhill, Seattle, WA. A simple tic-tac-toe design turns this record of Aiden's first fifteen months into a pleasingly organized page of simple shapes alive with bright colors and easy-to-read journaling.*

happy birthday 2 you!
September 9, 1997

Daddy helps Quinn
learn how to blow out
the candles. Daddy
has had a lot of
practice!!

your 2nd birthday
was low-key. We
celebrated with a
small party. Our
guests were Judy,
Jim and Jack,
Karen and Luanne
and Grandma
Carrell. We had
dinner, ice cream cake,
balloons and presents!

Good job, Quinn! you did it!

"Q"
turns

September 10, 1997

Quinn Turns
2 years old in
Des Moines, Iowa

Toys!
GLORIOUS TOYS!

Look at all these
presents — I can
hardly wait!

YIPeeeeee!!!

Quinn in his jammies
the morning of his birth-
day. He is playing with
all of his new toys from
his party the night before.
He got a lot of trucks
and emergency vehicles.

HAPPY BIRTHDAY

2

CHILDREN

Kids do the darnedest things! Before you know it, your child will be a teen, and those innocent days of discovery will be past. Don't miss the opportunity to record those precious years. Children's activities offer so many themes to choose from. Children play. They learn. Go off to school. Lose their baby teeth. Learn to ride a bicycle and skip rope. Learn to read and write. Develop friendships. Test boundaries. And all of it is done with individual style and filled with unique moments.

The possibilities for preserving these memories are as varied as the memories themselves. And these memory books help develop your child's self-esteem. They help children know who they are at an early age and instill a sense of security and worth. Why not create a storybook in which your child is the main character in a cast of family, friends, and pets? You may either write your own story or adapt a favorite one, substituting your child for the central character. Create a song book using pictures of your child to illustrate the words. Including early artwork will further personalize an album of your child's formative years, and delight her in the process.

This chapter features an interesting way to present children's portraits. Pages 38 and 39 outline a really neat technique that will give a 3-D effect to your pages, making your children's portraits seem to pop off the page. However you decide to save the history, you and your child will enjoy looking back to today.

▶ *CARYN LOVES HER ALFAFANATOR, by Joyce Feil, Littleton, CO. Caryn's affection for her horse and the relationship they have is extraordinary. The larger photograph allows us to see their mutual affection. The horse could not possibly wrap his neck around her any more* *than he has already. And no one will come between the two of them. The classically simple presentation allows the photos to speak for themselves. The arches make us feel as though we are looking into a barn stall at an everyday activity.*

KC

CARYN LOVES HER ALFAFANATOR

CREATE A PICTURE BOOK

Children love picture books. Little ones enjoy learning new words, talking about the pictures, or even making up stories of their own. Why not make a picture book with and about your child? An animal picture book is perfect for photos you've taken of your child at the zoo. Your child will learn animal names, and you'll both have fun creating the pages!

◄ TREE CLIMBERS, by Sandra Blair, Canyon Country, CA. What could be more natural than kids climbing trees on a bright spring day? The photos themselves become an extension of the trees they are in. Sandra has echoed the palette of the leafy branches in her bold artwork. Her trees look as natural as the real ones! And this she accomplishes using colored paper, stamps, and a sponge to add texture. Freehand touches provide additional texture to the tree trunks. Flower and insect stickers finish the page.

▲ APPLE SCHOOL DAYS, by Carrie Davis, Everett, WA. Children peering out from red, green, and golden apples bring smiles of remembrance of school days for all of us. This first-grade teacher more than met the annual challenge of how to incorporate individual school pictures into her scrapbook. The "apple" theme allowed her to include lots of photos in a small space. Photos were cropped with a circle template. The jaunty freehand-cut apples in a carefree arrangement give formal school portraits a new look.

◄ STICK FIGURE CLASS PHOTOS, *by Kim Buckley, Childress, TX. Preschoolers have energy to boot! Who says photos have to be large to make a point? This delightful page documents the year's activities in Kim's daughter's preschool class. The children's faces atop disarming stick figures drawn with pen suitably identify each one with name, age, and favorite activity. A perfect gift for the teacher.*

▼ A PROUD YOUNG ARTIST, *by Carey Van Druff, Santa Ana, CA.*

PRESERVING CHILDREN'S ARTWORK

If your child's drawing or painting is too large to include in your album, have a color photocopy made, reducing the image to fit the page. Silhouette cropping of the artwork emphasizes the handmade quality. Or you may want to include a photo of the actual item that was drawn or painted, as well as a photo of the young artist.

If you have a particularly prolific budding artist in your ranks, take a weekly or monthly photo of the child with the accomplishments of that period. This will give you a record of the growing child as well as the talent!

▶ TAKE THE TIME TO PLAY, by Tonia Jardine, Tacoma, WA. A scrapbook page can be a simple reminder of an important life lesson. Tonia says, "My two boys, their Grandma Jardine, and I were walking along Puget Sound when we came across a hopscotch etched in the boardwalk. I fell in love with the wise inscription and arrangement of the squares, so I took a couple of pictures to remember the design for my scrapbooks. It's a simple reminder of what's important in life."

TIP: PHOTO OP

Carry your camera with you to take advantage of opportunities to capture images that might suggest a theme for your scrapbook pages.

Best Buds...

allison
and
Josh

Playing with their
giga pets

Fall, 1997

3-D Elements

Bring depth to your pages with this 3-D technique. The process is simple and adds immeasurable interest. Select an area of a photo you want to emphasize. With this process a figure or group of figures, a flower—or anything you want—can be literally brought forward. It's really best to lay out your whole page before deciding which elements to emphasize. You might choose elements from various spots in the photo. And to create a balanced composition, you should see the whole scene ahead of time.

STEP 1.
Gather two copies of each photo that you want to make three-dimensional. Cut out the element you want to emphasize with the 3-D effect.

STEP 2.
Adhere generous amounts of double-sided padded adhesive to the backs of the silhouetted portions. Position the silhouetted portions on the uncut photograph in the same positions.

◀ *Best Buds, by Theresa McFayden, Omaha, NE.*

PUNCHES

Punch art adds even more dimension to this 3-D photo page. Punch art is easy to do, and with the large number of available punches and the many different papers available, the possibilities are astronomical! See Sources on page 116 for other images and information. You'll find punch art used on several pages throughout this book. For more instruction see pages 63 and 73. This project uses the following punches:

❖ *For Large Flowers—large circle, snipped for yellow flower*
❖ *For Large Flower Centers—small circle*
❖ *For Small Flowers—small circle*
❖ *For Small Flower Centers—1/4-inch round punch*
❖ *For Flower Leaves—birch leaf and small circle cut in half*
❖ *For Heart Accents—small and mini hearts*

▶▶ *(Overleaf)* HUGS AND KISSES TO THE SCARECROW, *by Donna Leicht, Appleton, WI. Lazy summer days on the farm. Hugs and kisses and more hugs and kisses as brother and sister take their turn greeting a treasured scarecrow. Each look at these cheery pages, with pictures of their favorite activities on the farm framed by summer-bright colored papers and even different colored checked borders, will bring happy memories of days in Door Country, Wisconsin, flooding back. The disarming photos are set off with bright colored mats.*

Hugs and Kisses to The Farm's Scarecrow!

Sarah loved this Lassie-like collie named Laddie. Laddie loved herding so much that she herded the baby chicks back into the chicken hut! This black pygmy goat was Sarah's favorite. She held him the entire week.

The currents are a little sour, but yummy!

More Hugs and Kisses to The Farm's Scarecrow!

Was this really how kids got water to drink in the olden days? It's fun!

LETTERING STYLES

Sometimes it's fun to experiment with different lettering styles. The bold lowercased alphabet (complete with a few backward letters) shown here is reminiscent of those used to teach the ABCs and is perfect for your children's scrapbook pages. Trace and use these or experiment with your own. The decorative alphabet included below can be copied by machine, or try copying this style freehand.

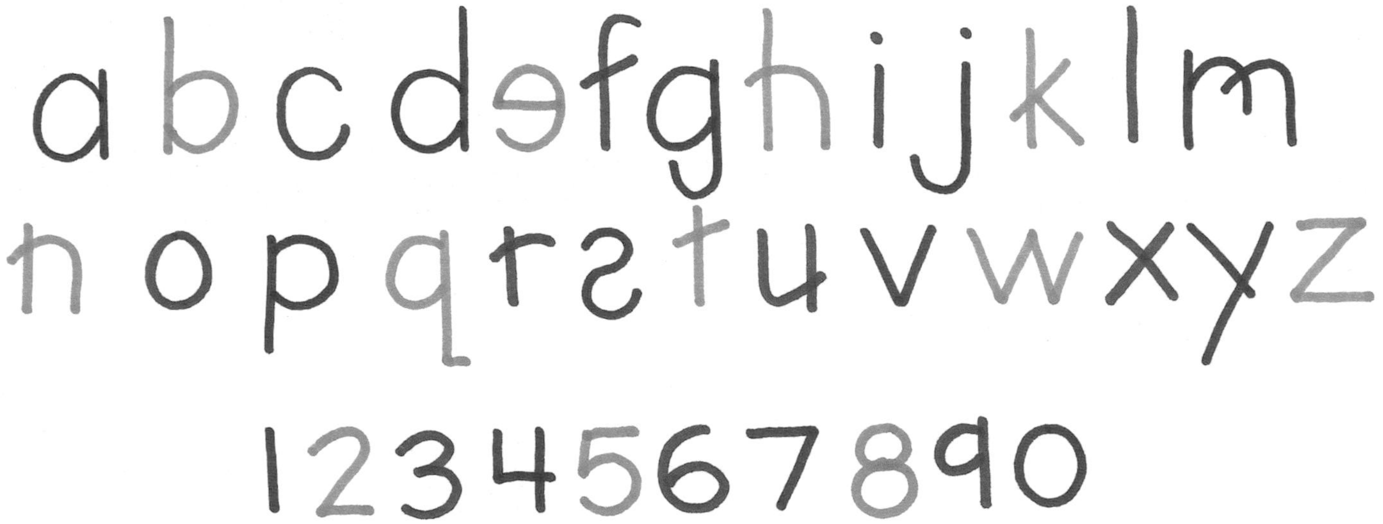

abcdefghijklm
nopqrstuvwxyz

1234567890

Letterstyle by Jennifer Johnston.

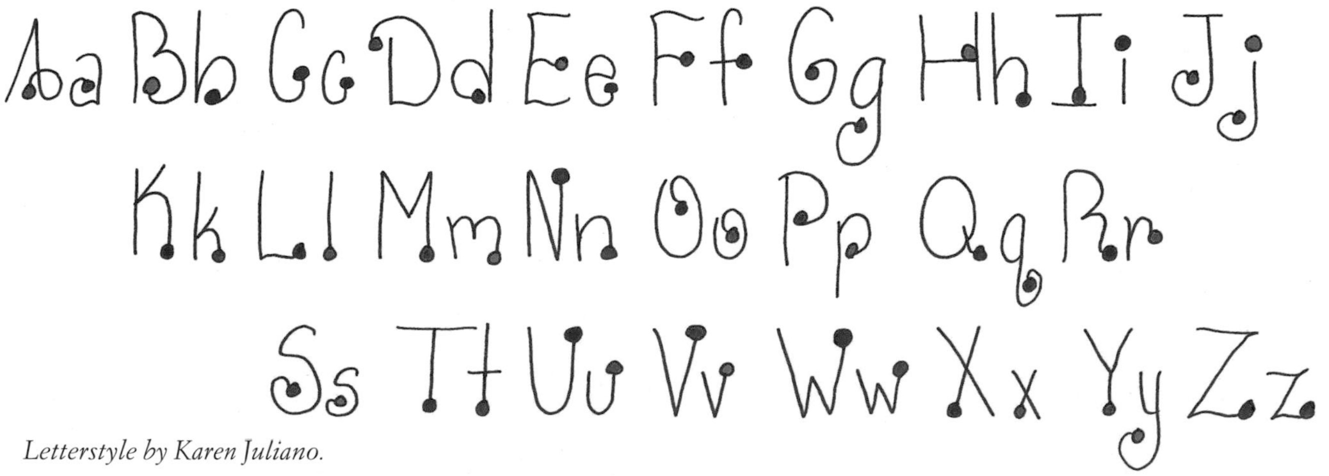

Aa Bb Cc Dd Ee Ff Gg Hh Ii Jj
Kk Ll Mm Nn Oo Pp Qq Rr
Ss Tt Uu Vv Ww Xx Yy Zz

Letterstyle by Karen Juliano.

▶ ROUGH & TUMBLE, *by Pam Klassen, Denver, CO. Photos by Alison Beachem. The playground is a natural place to take action shots of* your children and their friends. The "kids" lettering style, applied with different colored pens, accentuates the youthfulness of this page.

PETS

Whether small, large, furry, feathered, or scaly, pets enrich our lives and never fail to entertain. Their curious ways often volunteer them as the subject on the other side of a camera, and they always seem to outdo themselves with a new snapshot-worthy antic. Through their interesting personalities and achievements, or simply by virtue of their birth, pets hold an important place in family life. And for scrapbookers, that means a prominent place in the family photo album.

Photographing pets poses an interesting challenge—we've yet to find a dog who will obey the commands, "Sit, look pretty, and smile. Hold that." To help with that problem, we've included some tips for taking pet portraits on page 48. We've also included a how-to section on photo kaleidoscopes, an exciting technique that produces almost awe-inspiring results. Although the end products may look complex, don't be afraid to try.

The first "hello" from your feathered friend, your kitten's roll with a ball of yarn, your dog's graduation from obedience school—pet milestones are perfect fare for a scrapbook. If you have one or two pets, consider compiling pet-style baby books which record birth, significant firsts, and loving family members. If you have a large pet family, try making one spread for each member. Include the best pictures, write down factual information, journal about a funny memory. Your scrapbook can be one of the best ways to record for all just what your pets mean to you.

▶ MORGAN ST. CROIX, *by Sandra de St. Croix, St. Albert, Alberta, Canada. Some golden retrievers do know how to sit and pose regally for a portrait. Morgan St. Croix is one of them, and here he poses amid a mosaic-like pattern of tulip photos in his garden, basking in* *nature's bounty. The bright yellow and green freehand-cut letters spelling out his name tumble across the tulips. The garden photos are cropped in simple rectangular shapes creating a soft blanket of color around the master.*

CREATING PHOTO KALEIDOSCOPES™

Photo kaleidoscopes are "hands-on" art at its finest. Kaleidoscopes are intriguing and may seem complicated, but they are quick and simple to make using an equal number of regular and reversed photos.

▲ SOPHIE JEWELL, *page by Pam Klassen, Denver, CO.; kaleidoscope by Kathleen Paneitz, Longmont, CO. What better way to show off a furry friend than featuring her not once, but eight times! The effect is sophisticated, but the process is simpler than it looks.*

SELECT THE PHOTO

The most dramatic kaleidoscope effects are produced with photos that have repetitive patterns, intersecting lines, vivid colors, good light quality, and lots of activity.

DETERMINE CUTTING LINES

Place a clear plastic triangle (we've found that a 45-degree triangle is the easiest to work with) over the part of the photo you want to use. Place the edges on a part of the photo that will make an interesting pattern when matched with a reversed image. Holding a mirror against the side of the triangle can help you visualize this.

1. The original Sophie Jewell portrait.

DETERMINE NUMBER OF REPRINTS

Imagine the part of the photo you've chosen to use as a slice of pie. The angle you use will determine the number of slices needed; the angles must add up to 360 degrees, the number of degrees that make a circle.

ORDER REPRINTS

Have the photo lab make reprints of your original photo and the reversed image. If you decided to use a 45-degree angle, you'll need eight photos— four originals and four reversed images (a 60-degree angle needs 6 photos—3 originals and 3 reversed; a 30-degree angle needs 12 photos—6 originals and 6 reversed).

2. Eight copies of the original photo—four regular and four reversed. (Ask a photo shop to provide prints from your negatives.)

CUT PHOTOS

Lay the triangle over the part of the photo you want to use. Find at least three reference points that fall along the edge of the triangle and cut through these exact points on each original and reversed image photo.

ASSEMBLE CUT PIECES

Place one cut piece of an original beside one cut piece of a reversed image, matching along your reference points. Repeat with all pairs and assemble the pairs into a star.

ADD FINISHING TOUCHES

Trim the outside edge in a pleasing pattern. Mount the kaleidoscope on a scrapbook page using double-sided tape. Embellish the page as desired.

3. Using a 45-degree angle, crop the photos to create a pleasing pattern. Arrange in the shape of a star.

► BASKET OF PUPPIES, *by Nina Hershberger, Elkhart, IN.*

►► EMBER AT PISMO BEACH, *by Jennifer Jae Barber, San Jose, CA.*

▼ DAISY, *photograph by Jim Cambon, Fort Collins, CO.*

TAKING BETTER PET PORTRAITS

As with babies, photographing pets poses certain challenges because you can't just tell them to sit and smile for the camera. But with a little know-how, you'll get good results.

❖ *Select the right film. Choose fast film such as ISO 400 or 800 for clear action shots; use ISO 100 or 200 for stills.*
❖ *Choose a setting that accentuates your pet's personality and physical traits. For example, if your cat is a great lounger, you might photograph her in an easy chair, or stretched across a windowsill waiting for an unfortunate bird or mouse to venture forth.*
❖ *Clean and groom your pet before a sitting, possibly removing collars and tags.*
❖ *Take lots of photographs whenever you can. Your pet just might get used to it, and you'll have a better chance of getting some interesting shots.*
❖ *Don't be afraid of bribery. Small animal treats work wonders. Most professional animals are trained this way.*
❖ *You can control your pet's behavior. If you're quiet, chances are your pet will respond in a similar fashion.*

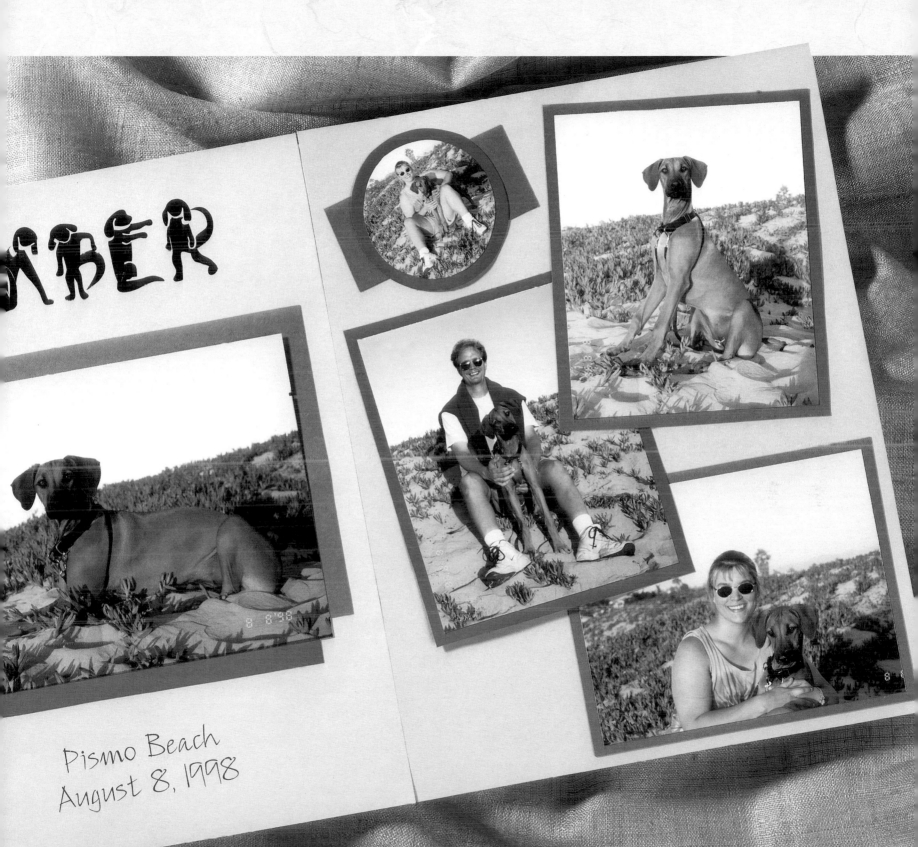

MBER

Pismo Beach
August 8, 1998

TEENS

You've come a long way, baby. Your "child" is now driving a car, earning a paycheck from an after-school job, soaring as an athlete, getting ready for the prom, thinking about and maybe even planning for the future. Perfect fodder for new scrapbook pages! Teen albums capture the years of constant change. They can also help teens recognize their strengths—perhaps even revealing future talents. Here are a few ideas for commemorating your child's teenage years.

A life album may summarize years one to eighteen and include birth, school days, and graduation. It could also include other important events such as a school play, a trip, an adventure with a special friend or grandparents, or a camping trip. You might also focus a teen album on one major activity such as sports, music, or theater. Activity albums allow you to focus on the details—documenting the span of a varsity football career could fill a hundred pages. A third option is to create a personal yearbook with social and academic highlights. A personal yearbook can tell the story of those memorable high school years from your teen's unique point of view. Page subjects might include passing her driver's test, the first date, induction into the honor society, a concert or recital, graduation, and awards.

There are as many techniques for producing your pages as there are possible themes. In this section we've included instructions for layered roses, just the thing for accenting a prom page, or commemorating any special event.

▶ *PINK DIAMOND SOCCER, by Claudia Hill, Whittier, CA. Creating a page devoted to your teen's favorite pastime, whether it be sports or another activity, goes a long way to building self-esteem. With sports,* *team colors are the way to go, and in this case what great colors those are! Take advantage of the available die cuts, stickers, and printed papers to make a unique and personalized page that says it all.*

AYSO 1993

◄ *SILVER DOLLAR FAIR, by Melisa Conwell, Orangevale, CA. Your teen has seen them at fairs, amusement parks, and shopping malls. And, no doubt, he or she has been in one of these contraptions more than once. Ask for the photo booth freeze frames and preserve these special mementos that might well include your teen's best friend. This page shows the same friends two years running and is embellished with a camera die cut.*

▼ *GOLF LESSON, by Jeanne Ciolli, Lake Forest, CA. Whether over, under, or right at par, most golfers take their time on the links very seriously. They look for improvement every time out, and they often find it. Photograph your teen striving for that perfect game. If you're lucky, you'll capture better and better strokes with each outing. This page was assembled with a scorecard, stickers, colored papers, and golf balls cut from a magazine.*

TEEN THEMES AND MEMORABILIA

Learning to drive, learner's permit, first car, copy of driver's license
Learning to change a tire
Locker decorations
Favorite teachers, coaches, mentors, and lessons learned from them
Special friends and family members
After-school jobs, first paycheck
Favorite clothes, fads, and munchies
Favorite places and hangouts
Applying for college, SATs, campus visits, top college picks
First date, dances, and proms
Current events and political interests
Bedroom decor
Weekend sleep schedule
Activities and achievements
Popular music, movies, and television programs
Changing hairstyles, first shave
Blank pages for friends to sign

◄ SKATEBOARD RAMP, *by Dianne Gottron, Hollister, CA. Playing with proportions and placement, Dianne has emphasized how high her son was skating—leaping tall buildings, soaring over treetops. Action shots such as these are favorites among teens and their parents alike. When looking at them in your scrapbook, you can almost hear the shouts of, "Look, Ma. No hands!" The houses, fence, and trees are freehand cut, and the ridges on the house and fence were created with an embossing stylus and ridged stencil.*

◄ BAND DAY, *by Jennifer Weeks, Tempe, AZ. Here's a wonderful example of how much a very simple page can express. These pages are some of Jennifer's first efforts, and we think they're very effective. When she cut the musical note from the blue background, she didn't want to just toss it, so she incorporated it into the design of the facing page. The note is freehand cut, and photos are cropped to complement that shape.*

▲ WHERE'S EVAN? *by Diane Stanley, Yorba Linda, CA. High school graduation is one of those exciting once-in-a-lifetime events that you will definitely want to capture on film. But it's easy to get carried away and find yourself with too many photographs that look a bit too similar. That's what happened here, and a page based on the* Where's Waldo *books is both humorous and practical. Extra photos are cut into triangles and arranged maze-like as borders around the page.*

▶ RYAN'S FIRST CAR, *by Carolyn Kissel, Bradenton, FL. Carolyn Kissel created a whole line of printed news items called "Seems Like Yesterday" to add historical journaling to her scrapbook pages. If you want to place your photos in an earlier time and place, try one of her products. (See Sources on page 116.) If your photos are current, use newspaper and magazine clippings to tell the story.*

I'M WEARING MY WHITE ROSE CORSAGE.

WEARING A BEADED BAG... A GLORIOUS ANTIQUE.

LOOKING BEAUTIFUL!

A HAPPY GRAD

CAITLYNN, HWIE LIE AND HER MOM
- PROUD MOM

YOU GUYS LOOK GREAT!

CHARLIE   VINCE   JEFF

GRAD '98

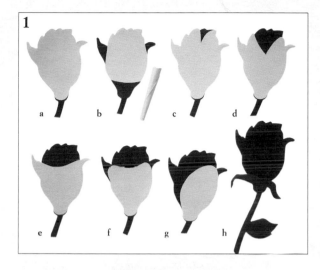

CREATING A LAYERED ROSE

This elegant three-dimensional flower was made using a commercially available flower die cut. (See Sources on page 116.) For one flower, you need eight identical rose die cuts—seven in the color of the petals and one in green for the stem. To add shading to the rose, purchase petal die cuts in two shades of the same color. Shape "a" shows what each die cut looks like at the outset. You will be cutting as shown to create the individual shapes to form the layered rose. All letters "a" through "h" in these instructions refer to the lettered images shown here, top left.

1. CREATE THE BASE

To create the base of the rose, trim die cuts "a" and "b" as illustrated, cutting away the portions shown in black. Roll die cut "b" cigar style and adhere to the middle of die cut "a." Set aside to dry.

2. TRIM DIE CUTS

Trim and adhere petals "c" through "g," cutting away the portions in black. Fold forward the tips of each petal, or use a round item such as a pen barrel to roll the tips forward. Layer and adhere the petals one on top of another on the base in order "c" through "g." Rounded petals will flatten out a little when stored in a scrapbook.

3. ADHERE THE STEM

To create the stem, trim die cut "h" as shown. Adhere the stem on top of the rose base. To add dimension to the stem, trim leaves from an extra green die cut and adhere them to your stem base. To add dimension to the stem and leaf, use an additional green die cut.

◄ *PRETTY IN PINK AND SILVER and PROM GUYS, by Linda Schell, North Vancouver, British Columbia, Canada. Roses are a special symbol in the life of Linda's daughter Cait. So Linda constructed roses in paper to embellish commemorative pages. The Pretty in Pink and Silver page uses rose-printed paper to echo the theme. The photos are triple-mounted with mats cut with fancy scissors, and silver rose stickers add the final touch. For Prom Guys, Linda freehand cut a "tuxedo" shape from printed and black and white papers. The red rose in the lapel is a dapper detail.*

HERITAGE

Margaret and Patti 1947 Marietta Ga.

There is no better gift you can give your family than their heritage, beautifully and accurately recorded for future generations. One of the most important elements of creating your heritage album is research. Read everything available about your family, and talk with older relatives about their memories. Each person will have a different perspective of the same event, so don't be surprised if you hear many versions of the same story! Use the information you collect for journaling—it will bring the pictures to life.

The other major element to gather for your album is photographs, and keeping them organized is vital. Consider starting an envelope for each member of the family to keep together all photos, documents, stories, and mementos relating to that person. If you have many group shots, make an envelope for each branch of the family.

Making the pages is next, and there is no right or wrong way to design your heritage album. Ask yourself a few simple questions. How much time and money do I want to invest? Are most of my photos from one era or do I have a mix of time periods? Do I want a simple or ornate design? The answers to these questions will help determine the direction of your design.

The technique of paper punch art on page 63 may be used to create many different styles of pages that can convey a specific time and place. We've seen many beautiful heritage pages over the years, and present only a few of our favorites here.

► *THE ROARING 20s, by Cheryl Thomas, Crackerjack Too, Highland, CA. Heirloom photos and stories hold a special place in the hearts of many of us, and making scrapbook pages with them is a special treat. The content, texture, and general feeling of this page bring the roar-* *ing 20s to life. The background paper used here is preprinted, but you could also make your own with genuine keepsake letters and a photocopy machine. The deep, rich, jewel-toned colors on this page add a sumptuous dimension and sophistication.*

The "ROARING" 20's

FREEDOM!

FUN!

FLAPPERS!

FORD!

HOW DID WE MEET?

◄ HOW DID WE MEET? *by Joyce Schweitzer, Greensboro, NC. Joyce is creating a scrapbook for her parents, and she mails them a new section of the book every few weeks as it is completed. Imagine the anticipation with which each package is opened! When her parents look back at the pictures and mementos, they recognize the glamour and the love in their marriage all over again. The simple techniques of paper cutting and matting used here evoke a very specific mood.*

► THE WHITAKER CHILDREN, *by Cheryl Thomas, Crackerjack Too, Highland, CA. Here is another use of the popular quilt theme for a page of old family photos. Designed to represent the simplicity of the old midwest, this page does just that. Shapes are punched from the yellow die cuts and four of the removed sections are used as corner decorations on the photograph. Drawn stitches and real buttons are delightful finishing details.*

►► FAMILY TREE, *by Allison Garmon, Jefferson, MD. Here's the result of blending two passions—genealogy and scrapbooking. Allison is fortunate enough to have photographs of ancestors as far back as six great-great grandparents. She even added a few branches for those grandparents for whom she did not have photos. Start your tree with a picture of yourself, and build back in time. An allover pattern of stamped leaves creates the background used here and the tree branches are drawn with a watercolor pen.*

The Roots of my Family Tree.

Allison Garman 1997

Margaret and Patti 1947 marietta, ga.

◀ VICTORIAN PICTURE FRAME, *by Marilyn Garner, San Diego, CA. This pretty assemblage of punch art has a bit of a Victorian flavor and is a great way to accent heirloom photographs. These flowers make use of fifteen different punches, and the result is both dressy and delicate. There is no limit to what you can do with punch art. Here the original punched shapes are hardly recognizable—the pieces are folded and combined with others to create uniquely styled flowers.*

Punch Art Frame

The simplicity of punch art has made it one of the most popular ways we know to create captivating pages. All you need are a few punches and some paper to make unique art for your scrapbook pages. Our paper artists marvel at how rapidly punch art projects take on a life of their own, adding charm and whimsy to scrapbook pages, photo frames, cards, invitations, and more. With a little imagination and a few punches, you can construct fabulous pages with extraordinary depth and dimension. Follow the steps below to construct the exquisite picture frame seen opposite.

STEP 1.

A small flower bud is constructed by snipping a small egg with a mini sun and layering it over another small egg, then layering it on top with a medium tulip.

STEP 2.

Portions of a small snowflake are layered over a small bell, then layered with a medium tulip to make a bell flower.

STEP 3.

A large flower bud is created by layering three small strawberries over a medium egg.

STEP 4.

To create tubular flowers, fold circles in thirds and layer with a tulip or bell and a portion of the snowflake.

TIP: KEEPING PUNCHES SHARP

When punches become dull, try punching through aluminum foil to sharpen. Or, to sharpen all edges, punch through a very fine grade of sandpaper in both directions (upside-down and right-side up).

Mosaic Beach Scene, by Denise Tucker, Versailles, IN. Photos from a beach vacation are cut and repieced into various sea-related shapes.

SPECIAL EVENTS

WEDDINGS

While your wedding may be a one-day, once-in-a-lifetime event, the opportunities for celebrating the occasion in your scrapbook are countless. Whether you're a bride-to-be or have celebrated milestone anniversaries, any time is a good time to plan or rethink your wedding album. Many of us spend vast amounts of time, energy, and money to make our wedding day a day unlike any other. And like everything related to this most special day, you want your wedding scrapbook to be exquisite, beautiful, breathtaking—in short, perfect.

There are as many different ways to style a wedding album as there are styles of weddings. If your wedding was simple and elegant, you may want your commemorative book to reflect that mood. If your wedding was colorful and gay, use bold pens and stickers to accentuate that tone. If your wedding took place years ago, consider creating an anniversary album that incorporates the theme or feeling of your wedding through the years since that day.

The pages shown opposite use simple, elegant frames to capture and preserve various moments of a wedding day. The scrapbook page featured on page 72 incorporates the technique of paper punch art to create a romantic setting for an heirloom wedding portrait. Punch art offers limitless options for creative expression. Literally hundreds of punches are available, and when you team them with boundless paper choices, you can create a page that is as unique as your experience. A book that captures the wonder of your wedding day will be treasured by you and your family for the life of the marriage and beyond.

▶ *WEDDING PORTRAITS, by Bev Klassen, Rosedale, British Columbia, Canada. These pages use simple, elegant frames to preserve memories of a daughter's wedding. The white frame featured on top is made from an embossed wedding invitation. You can create the right cropping for photos by matting with simple shapes. Freehand cut or use die cuts or punches to make flowers, buds, and leaves for the garland.*

Christine Suzanne Klassen and David Trenton Harms.
April 12, 1997.

Among the greatest
of the gifts God sends —
Are those special people
We can call our Friends.

Kevin Tancredo

8 Years Professional
Experience
• Wedding Cakes
• Special Occasions

Hm: 657-5538   Pg: 767-2639

▲ KEITH AND SARA, by LeNae Gerig, Hot Off The Press, Canby, OR. With printed papers and ribbon, this page captures all the softness and romance of the bride's attire. A printed paper was laid down for the background, and scalloped strips cut following the design of the lacy paper are used for borders top and bottom. A satin ribbon bow adds just a touch of dimension, and a matted card with journaling records the date.

TIP

Consider providing disposable cameras for the guests to use and leave at the tables.

◄ WEDDING CAKE, by Eileen Ruscetta, Westminster, CO. Very often, wedding guests come with their cameras and will send you their favorite snapshots of the party. When you add them to the thousands your photographer took, you may be overwhelmed. Here's a clever way to use all those extra photos—cut them up and create a mosaic border. This border is pieced together with dozens of 1/2-inch squares, and the effect mimics the lattice-work background of the featured photographs.

The Cake

▲ THE CAKE, *by Shelly Potter, Fairbanks, AK. Simple cropping and embellishing can speak volumes. The flower-covered arch at Shelly's reception inspired the shapes and design of this two-page spread of traditional cake-cutting activities. The border used here is preprinted, but you could also try drawing your own based on your photographs. A combination of many small stickers could also provide just the right touch. And don't forget the wonderful effects that can be created with fancy scissors.*

◄ WEDDING DANCERS, *by Kathleen Phelan, Baltimore, MD. If you're lucky, you may get a fabulous candid photograph from your wedding party like this one taken by photojournalist Perry Thorsvick. This shot is full of love and celebration, and is enhanced by simple embellishments. The ribbon border is created with colored pens and a wavy ruler. Simply draw one line, then move the ruler a bit to the right and draw another line. Connect the ends and color in.*

TIP: CROP IT RIGHT

When photographing people for your scrapbook page, get in close and keep your design simple.

Pictures at the

Ritz Carlton

Our photographer was Trish from Skinner-Vaughn Photography. As a special offer, she took us downtown two days before the wedding for some special pictures. These photos were taken at the Ritz Carlton Hotel on the Plaza. We also had pictures taken at the Nelson Atkins Art Gallery. Everyone we met treated us like king and queen.

▲ RITZ CARLTON, by Ann Perry, Allen, TX. Friends and family members who weren't able to attend Ann's wedding say that looking through her album makes them feel as if they were there. Simple die cuts like the dove and heart used here convey a message of love and peace. Adding lots of journaling throughout the album will also help to tell the story of the day in its entirety, allowing loved ones to more fully realize the event. The decorative-edged frames for the photos add a romantic touch.

▶ ▶ (Overleaf) WHITE-ON-WHITE WEDDING PAGE, by Pam Klassen, Denver, CO. The beautiful punch art on this page creates a truly romantic setting for an heirloom wedding portrait. Creating the right ambiance for your photos goes a long way to telling their stories. And while this treatment may look complicated, it's done with only three punches. The instructions presented on page 73 tell you all you need to know to create punch art backgrounds that will be perfect for your scrapbook pages.

PUNCH ART

Punch art can extend your scrapbooking budget by making good use of paper scraps that might otherwise be thrown away. With this project, punched art is used as delicate detailing providing a romantic soft white background on which the elegant historical photograph is presented. To make the delicate white-on-white background shown opposite, you need only three punches: a large circle, a small fleur-de-lis, and a diamond extension.

FLOWERS

Here we've combined two punched shapes to create a third. For each flower:

Step 1. Punch one shape using the diamond extension punch.

Step 2. Punch six fleur-de-lis shapes.

Step 3. Position the six fleur-de-lis shapes in a circle around a diamond and the flower is complete.

SWIRLS

We created crescents using a simple technique which we call offset punching. For each swirl:

Step 1. Punch one large circle from a sheet of paper.

Step 2. Flip the punch upside down and offset previously punched circle to create a crescent-shaped piece.

Step 3. Continue cutting crescents from the edge of the primary circle.

Step 4. Position the crescents on the page in alternating directions.

▼ *FLEUR-DE-LIS BORDER, by Debbie Hutchings, Longmont, CO. For this border we've combined multiples of the same shape to create a new one. Simply arrange four small fleur-de-lis shapes in a circle to create a flower. Connect the flowers to make a border.*

TRAVEL

No two things go more hand-in-hand than travel and picture taking. For many people, foreign travel is a once-in-a-lifetime opportunity that yields a much different vacation than hitting the local beach or visiting with family. That's not to say we have to go abroad to find memories that we'll treasure—your dream vacation may be in the next state, or even the next town. Wherever your travels may take you, there is no better way to preserve and later remember the splendor of the architecture, experiences, and people away from home than in a scrapbook.

The scrapbook page shown opposite uses simple borders created with paper and punches to mimic the architecture found in the American Southwest. Cutting and layering paper is a great way to create a page that represents the climate, terrain, and "feel" of your vacation spot. Take a good look at the interesting paper-layering technique presented on pages 84 and 85—it's almost as good as being there.

In addition to landmarks, take pictures of more ordinary sights—details of carvings in a church, a colorful garden, or even a local fruit-market vendor will add visual impact to your scrapbook. Collect memorabilia such as postcards, brochures, ticket stubs, postage stamps, currency, newspapers, and maps. Keeping a detailed journal of your travels will help you identify the sites you've photographed and add details the camera can't capture. Armed with your photos, memorabilia, and travel journal, you can relive the journey while creating your memory album.

► *CANYON ROAD INDIAN MARKET, by Debbie Hutchings, Longmont, CO. This page has the look and feel, almost the temperature, of the Southwest. Using only two punches, Debbie created borders that reflect the architecture in her photographs. For the top border, the top part of a small cross is punched into opposite sides of a paper strip. The same punch is used at an angle to create mats for lettering, and the page is finally embellished with the leftover bits from a southwest border punch.*

Canyon
Road
Indian
Market

Santa fe
New Mexico

▲ CANYON LANDS NATIONAL PARK, *by Wendie Waldman, Silver City, NM. The vista in this national park is breathtaking, and well captured in these stunning photographs. Because the photographs are so open and inviting, keeping the pages that hold them fairly simple makes them seem even more vast. The muted color of the background paper provides an ideal base for these stunning images. Using embossing powder and rubber stamps, you can create textured images that will complement all kinds of photographs and styles of scrapbook pages.*

Within the scrapbook photo lettering:

WALNUT CANYON

February 1996

The Sinagua Indians lived in these cliff dwellings. They were built sometime around 1125-1250.

Sinagua in Spanish means "without water"

Walnut Canyon was an important & populated Indian community.

We walked ¾ of a mile & climbed 185' to an elevation of 7000'. We saw 25 cliff dwelling rooms+ were able to walk through them.

▲ WALNUT CANYON, by Debbie Schubert, Phoenix, AZ. Photo letters is a technique that we love because it is so versatile. You can use it to create everything from fun and funky scrapbook pages to quiet and elegant ones. You may use purchased letter stencils or freehand your own unique alphabet. The technique is especially useful if you have many photographs from the same place. It's also an opportunity to use any less-than-perfect photographs that your children may have taken. A simple trim will turn them into works of art.

TIPS FOR LETTERING TECHNIQUES

❖ Practice makes perfect! If you are writing the letters freehand, you need to practice so you can feel the arc of the letters in your hand. If you are freehand cutting the letters out of cardstock or photos, practice with blank paper first.

❖ Keep the size of your page in mind when selecting letter style and size. Choose letters that will fit the space size and shape.

❖ When selecting a lettering style, always choose one that fits the tone of your page. Each style has its own personality.

❖ Experiment by writing the same word or phrases with several different pens and pen nibs to find one that feels comfortable and produces an appropriate lineweight for your page. Try a variety of styles.

❖ Plan ahead! Always sketch out the lettering out on scrap paper before fixing it to your page. If you are going to cut the letters freehand, cut them out of scrap paper first and lay them on your page, moving them around until you find the right spot and angle.

▲ VICTORIA, *by Denise M. Johnson, Vancouver, WA. A map of the area visited makes a great background for travel photos. When you are using letters as graphic elements on a page, what they look like is as important as what they say. This bold cut-out "Victoria" announces itself in bright blue to match the background color. The cohesive page is a delightful remembrance of a colorful trip.*

◄ NEW YORK CITY, *by Eileen Ruscetta, Westminster, CO. For those who live in small or rural communities, a trip to the Big Apple is sure to be unforgettable. And here is yet another use of paper cutting—you can use black paper with silver and gold to create a whole skyline at night.*

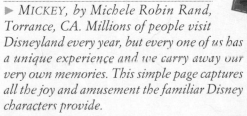

▶ MANHATTAN POCKET PAGE, *by Becki Spivey, Lubbock, TX. A pocket page is perfect for preserving all the memorabilia we can't seem to avoid collecting every time we travel to a new destination. Maps, brochures, and museum guides will help us remember many details we may otherwise forget over the years. Here, tucked into a half pocket on the scrapbook page, the material is actually usable. Items can be easily removed for use and then returned for safekeeping.*

▲ NEW ORLEANS, *by Trisha Wesler, King of Prussia, PA. If you didn't pick up a map of the area for your scrapbook, you can re-create the topography by making a collage of extra photographs. For this page, Trisha simply traced the outline of the state of Louisiana from an atlas and then filled in the pencil outline with photos cut to fit and arranged within the shape.*

▶ MICKEY, *by Michele Robin Rand, Torrance, CA. Millions of people visit Disneyland every year, but every one of us has a unique experience and we carry away our very own memories. This simple page captures all the joy and amusement the familiar Disney characters provide.*

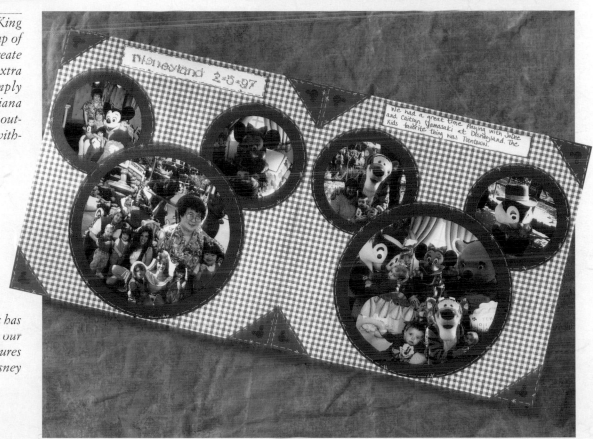

Photo kaleidoscopes never fail to amaze and intrigue us, no matter how many different versions we've seen. While the technique may look difficult because of the complex-looking results, don't be intimidated. With a few good photographs and a few simple tools, such as a triangle or protractor and a craft knife, you too can create enchanting works of art. See page 46 for more information on how to design photo kaleidoscopes.

▲ *EIFFEL EMBRACE, by Gordon Gerbrandt, Denver, CO. Photograph by Deborah Mock. This is a classic twelve-piece photo kaleidoscope made from 3 1/2 x 5-inch photos using a 30-degree angle.*

▲ *VERSAILLES CHAPEL CEILING PANORAMA, by Gordon Gerbrandt, Denver, CO. Photograph by Deborah Mock. This is a classic eight-piece photo kaleidoscope made from 3 1/2 x 5-inch photos using a 45-degree angle.*

▶ *SASHA'S FAN, by Gordon Gerbrandt, Denver, CO. Photograph by Michele Gerbrandt. This clever eighteen-piece photo kaleidoscope uses eighteen photos cut with a 20-degree angle.*

▲ ORIENTAL GARDEN, *by Angela Pechin, Gilroy, CA. If you're not ready to dive into the photo kaleidoscopes described on the preceding pages, here's a technique that may warm you up to the idea. The fan used here is the perfect environment for scenic photographs of Singapore. To make a pattern, photocopy and enlarge the fan shown here to desired size. Cut the entire shape from one piece of paper, then cut two sections of a contrasting color. Crop your favorite photos to fit the fan sections. Freehand cut a tassel and attach it with drawn cords.*

TIPS FOR FOOLPROOF JOURNALING

❖ Write text freehand with a very light pencil, using a ruler for placement and alignment. Trace over the outline of the finished text with colorful pens and markers. Always use pigment-ink pens, which won't fade over time.

❖ To practice, journal on a separate piece of paper, then cut it out and mount it on the page with your photos.

❖ Use a lettering template and a light pencil to trace your writing directly onto your scrapbook page. Highlight with colorful pens and markers.

❖ Type your message on your computer using a fancy font and appropriate point size. Crop the printout, mat it, and mount it onto your page. Or trace the message onto your page using a light box.

❖ Inscribe die cuts or mats, or write around your photos in curved lines. Write inside the outline of a template, turning paragraphs into interesting shapes.

This area of french countryside was on the Napoleon Highway. It was beautiful. Here we stopped for one of our famous picnic lunches. This was our view!

FRANCE

Our first experience in france was at MCDONALDS. We were all starving for "real food." It tasted so good.

It took us 12 hours to drive from Switzerland to France. It wasn't the distance, but the windy, hilly roads. We all hated to ride in the back seat because we were so carsick!

▲ FRANCE, *by Lisa Wight, Derwood, MD. Sometimes our travels, no matter how exotic, trigger a bit of homesickness. The cure? Find something familiar, whether it be a book, a movie, or a good old-fashioned hamburger. Go ahead and remember that in your scrapbook, too. A page like this one will bring back a lot of memories and perhaps cause a few chuckles in years to come.*

▶ EIFFEL TOWER, *by Cheryl Parton, San Juan Capistrano, CA. The Eiffel Tower is such a strong symbol of Paris that when you open a scrapbook page with its likeness, there can be no doubt where you were.*

▶ UNDER THE SEA, *by Sandy Holly, Laguna Hills, CA. A good, sharp knife is to a paper artist what a brush is to a painter. This three-dimensional, layered fish seems to swim across the page.*

LAYERED PAPER CUTTING

Use colored paper, circle cutter or templates, cutting mat, a craft knife, stickers, and pens, and follow the steps outlined here to bring your ideas to life. A pattern for the cutout design can be sketched freehand or assembled from various commercial templates on a piece of scrap paper. Be sure to draw enough cutout sections along the outline of your design so that it can be easily distinguished.

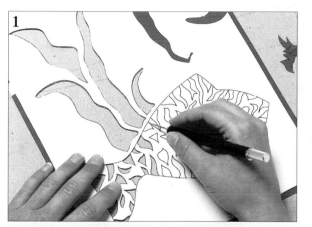

STEP 1.

Lay your page over a cutting mat. Place your pattern in the desired position. Cut out each section using your pattern as a guide. Remove the pattern and make additional cuts as desired until you are happy with the design.

STEP 2.

Place the page over a second color of paper on top of the cutting mat. Cut out sections of the second layer as desired. The areas you cut out will reveal a third color of paper.

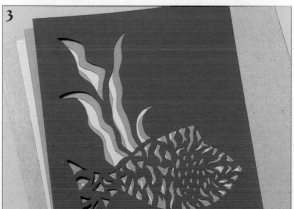

STEP 3.

To assemble the design, adhere the cutout page to the second cutout layer. Then adhere the second layer to a third, solid layer.

COLOR

❖ *The colors in your photos will provide the information you need to choose colors for the other components of your scrapbook page—background paper, mats, and any additional decorative devices.*

❖ *Colors can convey different feelings or moods. Red is exciting, blue is tranquil, yellow is cheerful, green represents the "natural world." Decide what feeling or mood you want your scrapbook page to elicit in the viewer. Or what are you saying with the page? How do you feel about it?*

❖ *Select a color in the photo that you want to emphasize, and use shades or tones of it in the background paper, mats, and other decorative materials.*

❖ *Many holidays and the seasons have colors associated with them. You can play with subtle variations on the basic colors for a more unusual sophisticated look.*

❖ *Look at a color wheel to help you select color combinations for your scrapbook pages.*

❖ *Experiment by laying your photos on different color background papers to find the effect you like.*

❖ *Too many colors on a page is distracting.*

FALL 1998, by Cassie Brumbaugh, Visalia, CA.

Fall 1998 ~

THROUGH THE YEAR

The changing of seasons creates new and fascinating photo opportunities year after year after year. When the first crocus peeks out from beneath the snow, it sets the stage for all the wonderful rites of spring that will follow. The dog days of summer are filled with baseball, lemonade stands, and stolen moments spent napping in the hammock. Autumn leaves bring us back to school or out to a tailgate party before the big football game. And winter delivers the magic of the holidays and, in the colder climates, all kinds of games to be played with the funny white stuff. Why not commemorate your favorite seasonal events in a book of their own?

Each season has its own color palette and symbols, offering excellent opportunities for creative borders and accents. A page of rust, gold, burgundy, and brown will leave no doubt about the time the page celebrates. A snowflake may be the perfect frame for your favorite winter face. The pages that follow incorporate many of our old favorite techniques along with some brand-new ones, such as the exciting paper folding technique featured on pages 98 and 99. Paper folding is another technique that may not seem natural to scrapbooking at first, but is one that opens up a fascinating world of possibilities. And what a wonderful use of those colored and printed papers .

Whatever the seasonal slant, take advantage of all the inspiration that Mother Nature and your fellow scrapbookers have to offer to create your own special book for all seasons.

▶ *GARDEN MOSAIC, by Sandra de St. Croix, St. Albert, Alberta, Canada. We've found that many scrapbookers also enjoy cooking, other crafts, and gardening as well. If you love your garden, creating a photo mosaic like this one allows you to enjoy your flowers all year long. For this effect, simply trim a photo into uniform squares and arrange the squares with a little bit of space between each one. Repeat with as many photos as will fit. This page is a reconstruction of garden scenes using one-inch squares. The finished effect is stunning.*

Heritage Trail

▲ ANNA IN BLACK AND WHITE, *by Jenny Johnson, Bakersfield, CA. You can create a garden in your scrapbook even without garden photography. Just use stickers! The soft black-and-white photos are accented with colorful flower and butterfly stickers, which provide a special garden patch for Anna, who Jenny calls her "little bug."*

◄ SMILING SUNSHINE BOY, *by Charlotte Wilhite, Fort Worth, TX. The smile says it all here, and what better way to accentuate that warmth than with sunny printed paper? Many photographs exude a specific quality or emotion, and it's great fun to come up with a page that reflects that feeling. Here we've also used embossing powder on the corner mounts for an extra glow. Sprinkle the powder on the mounts and apply heat with a heat gun until the ink shines.*

◄◄ HERITAGE TRAIL, *by Janice Wiers, Merrimack, NH. Here's another type of mosaic that features scenic photographs. This page is a good way to use quite a few landscape photos and still highlight the most important subject—in this case, Benjamin. Arrange an even number of photos in a grid to cover your page, and crop your featured photo into an oval for the center. Here we've used fancy scissors and colored paper to make a mat, then we've added accents with a silver pen.*

Smell
Grandma's Prize
Geranimums

Small Animal Day at MSU
was great. I got to hold
chicks & ducks. Watched
mother pig feed her babies.
Holly Beers & Steve came
with us.

~World
of
Wo

Beep!
Beep!

PIECING PAPER GERANIUMS

STEP 1.

For each full bloom, cut three colors of petals using the template we've provided. Intertwine the three petals as shown. For centers, layer silhouette flower punches cut from two different colors. Use the petal template to cut large geranium leaves from some different shades of green. For half blooms, freehand cut the petals. For the center, punch a scalloped oval and trim.

STEP 2.

For buds, punch the heart from the petal color. Punch green scalloped oval, then trim and layer as shown.

This page is finished with freehand cut stems as well as a large flowerpot and spiral punches, a rooster die cut, and lots of dots and squiggles.

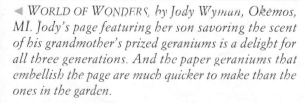

◄ WORLD OF WONDERS, by Jody Wyman, Okemos, MI. Jody's page featuring her son savoring the scent of his grandmother's prized geraniums is a delight for all three generations. And the paper geraniums that embellish the page are much quicker to make than the ones in the garden.

LEAVES ♥ PUMPKINS ♥

HOMEMADE PIES ♥

FALL

Sunday, Sept. 20, 98 - Grammy, Michael & I went apple picking. We picked 6 apples & ate 3. It was extremly hot in the orchard so we didn't stay long.

KIMBALL FRUIT FARM

SQUASH EGGPLANT PIES

♥ SCARECROWS ♥ ACORNS ♥

APPLE PICKING • ♥ RAKING ♥

JAM   JELLY

TURKEY DINNERS

AUTUMN ♥   ♥ HARVEST ♥

JAKE HAD A GREAT
TIME RUNNING
THROUGH THE
CORNFIELD
AND
CHOOSING
HIS OWN
PUMPKIN.

WE WENT TO
AT LOMBAR
WANTED
AND WA
ABOUT

WHEN WE WENT WITH THE PRESCHOOL,
THE KIDS WERE TOLD TO PICK
ONE THE SIZE OF THEIR HEAD.

OCT '97

OCT '99

◀◀ (*Previous spread*) FALL QUILT, *by Lisa Button, Billerica, MA. Lisa sat at the dining room table thumbing through magazines looking for inspiration for a fall scrapbook page. Staring out into space, she noticed a cross-stitch sampler she had made, and that sparked the idea for this page, which won first prize in a local scrapbooking contest. Inspiration is every-where, and there's a lot to be found in other crafts you may enjoy. Create quilt blocks of col-ored and printed papers and place mounted photos in the squares. Embellish your quilt with die cuts, stickers, and shapes from paper punches. You can trace things like the letter-ing from jam jars and other sources using a light box.*

▲ FALL, *by Charlotte Wilhite, Fort Worth, TX. Close-ups of ferns, flowers, water, gravel, bark, or cloudy skies can make strong statements when used as elements on your page. And they can set the mood or the season without detracting from your photographs. Here we've cut photos of fall leaves into one-inch strips and created a border for a two-page spread. The freehand-cut leaves used for journaling accentuate the seasonality of the page.*

◀ JAKE AND THE SCARECROW, *by Liz Kajiwara, Palmdale, CA. These pictures of Jake in a pumpkin patch leave no doubt that autumn has arrived. There are many seasonal printed papers available, such as the scarecrow paper used here, and you can use other plain and printed papers to mimic an element from your chosen paper. The pumpkins are freehand cut from a light orange paper and sponged with orange stamping ink for added dimension. Stickers and journaling complete the page.*

PAPER FOLDING

Paper folding is one of the most exciting things that ever happened to scrapbook art. With a few folds here, a few tucks there, and some creative assembly, you can frame your photos with paper art that is reminiscent of origami. And it's easy to do. There are many different folds you can use—here we present the envelope fold. By assembling folded pieces in a ring, you can create a round frame. Altering the number of folded pieces and assembly method can yield square frames, or smaller wreaths with no openings to use as embellishments. Do some experimenting. Once you start paper folding, you won't want to stop. To create the wreath shown here, you'll need twenty-five 3 x 3-inch squares of lightweight paper. Fold each piece following the instructions for the envelope fold. Try folding a practice piece first.

Paper folding technique by Kris Mason and Laura Lees.

ENVELOPE FOLD

1

A   B

C   D

2

3

Do not
crease edge

4

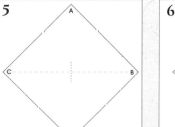

5

A
C   B
D

6

A
C
D

STEP 1.
Label the backside of your practice piece as shown.

STEP 2.
Fold A to D and crease the diagonal edge.

STEP 3.
Fold B to C, but do not crease the edge.

STEP 4.
Pinch the top of the triangle as shown.

STEP 5.
Unfold the square.

STEP 6.
Fold B to center pinch mark.

STEP 7.
Fold D to A.

STEP 8.
Fold C to center pinch mark.

STEP 9.
Fold C back up to E.

STEP 10.
Insert a pencil into the last fold to create a pocket.

STEP 11.
Flatten the pocket to form a small kite shape.

TO ASSEMBLE THE WREATH

First cut out a circle with an outer diameter of seven inches and an inner diameter of five inches (measurements will vary depending on the size of your photograph). Beginning with one folded square, "kite"-side up and point-side down, attach a small piece of double-sided tape to the front as shown. Place the next folded square on top of the one with the tape so that the bottom point of the new kite is just to the right of the previous kite. Repeat all the way around the ring, tucking the last piece under the first to finish.

7

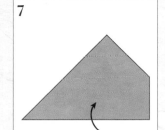

8

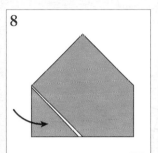

9

E

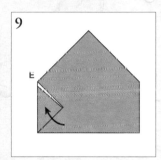

10

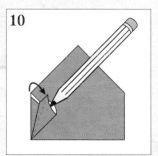

11

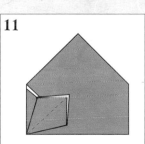

◄ SNOWY TIMES, WARM HEARTS, by Joyce Hill Schwietzer, Greensboro, NC. Joyce and her daughter are dueling scrapbookers, working side by side. Here's what one snowy afternoon can produce. The snowflakes are cut from white cardstock with a scallop scissors. You can use the snowflakes as mats for photos or simply to embellish a page. The Christmas trees are also cut from white cardstock, and the printed paper in the background adds even more snow to the scene.

◄ ONCE UPON A SNOWY DAY, *by Joellyn Borke Johnston, Des Moines, IA. The first snowstorm in a new home adds wonder to an already wonderful time. If you're lucky and haven't packed the camera away too deep in a box, you'll be ready to capture the moment on film. Lace paper makes a textured snowy background, and the letters are cut from white paper and decorated with a snowflake stamp and ink. Punched snowflakes add the final touch.*

▲ SNOWFLAKE PICTURE FRAME, *by Pam Klassen, Denver, CO. Seize the fun of winter's first snow with a giant snowflake. The heart inset will hold six of your favorite small photos. This snowflake pattern is just one of many found in* Paper Snowflakes for All Ages *(see Sources on page 116). Use the template provided here to trace the outline of the snowflake onto your white paper. Using small scissors with sharp points, carefully cut out the silhouette and the six heart shapes. Mount small portraits behind the hearts.*

HOLIDAYS

Holidays provide wonderful material for theme scrap-books. These special days, filled with family and friends, offer photo opportunities that only come around once a year. There are lots of holiday materials available to the scrapbook artist—stickers, print-ed papers, die cuts, special borders, and other seasonal decorations—making it easy to create unique pages in whatever amount of time you have available. Most holidays also have a partic-ular color scheme, so simply using several colors of paper can set the mood.

Holidays are often full of surprises, and that's why we've included instructions in this sec-tion for creating window or lift-the-flap pages and pop-ups. Open the window of a countdown calendar or turn the page of your scrapbook to a pop-up page and discover something unexpected. We've also included a list of 25 things to do with printed paper, enough to take you through all the year's holidays and more.

When creating photographic memories of holiday gatherings, take time to write about the people, activities, or things that make this time of year special. Perhaps food is a major attraction at your get-togethers. If so, why not include recipes of traditional or your favorite dishes? Birthdays may be accompanied by gifts; consider writing a list of special presents. Whether you're celebrating one of the big hol-idays such as Christmas or Hanukkah, or even an esoteric one such as Groundhog Day, take the time to collect the very special memories that are so unique to these times.

▶ *CHRISTMAS TREE, by Joyce Feil, Littleton, CO. One year the Feil family made a tree-gathering journey into the forest to cut down their own Christmas tree. The whole family wandered around in the forest searching for the perfect tree. When they all agreed they had found* *it, all three children helped cut it down. It was the youngest child's job to yell "timber." And they remember the day in full detail when-ever they look at this commemorative scrapbook page. The frame is a die cut, and the hearts are punched.*

GINGERBREAD HOUSE

For children, the weeks before Christmas can seem like an eternity, punctuated by the question, "How many days until Christmas?" A countdown calendar helps make the days fly by. Consider involving older children in creating this delightful gingerbread house, or make it for them as a surprise.

▲ *GINGERBREAD HOUSE, by Pam Klassen, Denver, CO. Bright-colored stickers adorn this holiday calendar starring Santa and Mrs. Claus centerstage. There is a lift-the-flap window to open every day from the first of December leading up to Christmas.*

TIP: MAKE IT LAST

To make your calendar more durable, use a heavy card-stock for constructing the house.

STEP 1. CUT OUT THE HOUSE

Photocopy and enlarge the house pattern on page 118. Place the pattern on brown cardstock over a cutting mat. Using a craft knife and straight edge, cut along the dotted lines through both the pattern and cardstock. Using an embossing stylus, make an indentation along the fold lines for the windows and doors. Fold open.

STEP 2. MARK AND DECORATE THE OPENINGS

Lay the cutout house on your page and lightly pencil the position of each opening. Lay the house aside. Create a scene for each window—use Christmas photos, stickers, and die cuts, or freehand-draw an object or write a message.

STEP 3. DECORATE THE HOUSE

Mount the house on the page, being careful to correctly position the window openings. Write the appropriate number or date on the front of each window. Decorate the gingerbread house as desired, using the example as a guide.

▲ *GLORIA POP-UP, by Erica Pierovich, Longmont, CO.*

A Pop-Up Primer

We love pop-ups. For not as much work as you might imagine, you can create a unique, special page for just the right occasion. One might think that an interactive page would have no place in a scrapbook, but that is definitely not the case. You can create marvelous pop-up pages that sit nicely in your scrapbook. The pop-up we include here offers an album spread decorated with layers of paper and die cuts along with silhouetted photos. The pop-up section is attached to the top of the page. Silhouette cut photos and follow the instructions below to create a pop-up page. Freehand cut the angel wings, harp, and trumpet.

STEP 1. CREATING THE BASE

Use a photocopier to enlarge the base pattern on page 118, or draw your own to fit your album. Cut the base from sturdy paper; fold in half, then fold flaps up. Use a straight edge to make sharp creases. If the base template is wider than your paper, cut out each side separately. Join these two pieces and reinforce the seam from behind with a one-inch strip of paper.

STEP 2. DECORATE THE BASE

Lay the pop-up base in place so you can see what parts of the page are covered or visible. Now decorate your pop-up completely, including all journaling, before mounting it on the page. For added interest, let some of the decorative elements extend above the top of the pop-up base. When decorating the center fold, leave enough "give" to allow the seam to expand and contract. Stickers do not work well. You may want to place the decorations on either side of the center fold.

STEP 3. MOUNT THE POP-UP

Position it with the center fold along the center of the gap between two pages. Close the pages to make sure the pop-up doesn't protrude outside the pages. Trim to fit if necessary.

STEP 4. ADHERE THE POP-UP

Apply two rows of adhesive to the flaps and adhere them to the pages at a 45-degree angle. The outside edges of the base will be flush at some point with the top edge of the two pages.

▲ HAPPY HANUKKAH, *by Karyn Noskin, Calabasas, CA. Here's a simple way to combine many nights of celebrations onto one page. First cut candles and flames of colored paper using fancy scissors. Cut your photos to the same shape as the candles, just a bit smaller. Mount the photos and embellish the page with stickers and lettering. This idea is perfect for a holiday of several days. But it may also serve well for many other kinds of memory pages. For a totally different idea, you could use this technique to celebrate your child's birthday parties. Or early first-days-of-school.*

▶ HANUKKAH COUNTDOWN, *by Pam Klassen, Denver, CO. The window-a-day idea is popular with children who are anxious for the holidays to arrive. This page is constructed differently from the gingerbread house on page 104, but the effect is similar. In fact, this construction is simpler and offers an opportunity for creating with children. Cut rectangles of colored paper for the candle bases. Fold the bases in half and mount photos on the inside right of each. Mount the candles on the page, adding a freehand cut flame for each. Add freehand cut dove and Star of David, and journal a prayer or other special phrase.*

Blessed art Thou, O God our Lord,
Who made us Holy with His word,
And told us on this feast of light,
To light one candle more each night.
~Jessie E Sampter

► JELLY BEANS & EASTER EGGS, by Cindy Barents, Redlands, CA. Easter is a time for new beginnings and offers a wonderful opportunity to begin collecting family memories in a scrapbook. The egg is a great shape for creating an Easter photomontage such as the one shown here. Lightly pencil a large oval on your page, then crop and piece your photos to fit the oval. Embellish with stripes, zigzags, and diamonds cut from colored paper. The spirals, eggs, and hearts are punched, and there's always room for stickers.

◄ EASTER 97, by Trenna Hart, Kaneohe, IL. Trenna has taken the popular craft of egg painting for Easter and put it to work on this scrapbook page. Begin with egg shapes cut from plain colored or white paper and decorate the eggs with colored pencils and pens, stickers, punch art, whatever you please. Decorating paper eggs for your scrapbook is another great way to involve children in the process—just give them some paper and pencils and let them create!

25 THINGS TO DO WITH PRINTED PAPER

by Anne Wilbur

1. *Buy it.* Don't stop until you have one of everything.
2. *Organize it.* File by color, pattern, or theme.
3. *Trade it.* Organize a printed paper swap meet.
4. *Wallpaper it.* Use a whole sheet as background.
5. *Frame it.* Create interesting mats for your photos.
6. *Mat it.* Choose a vivid solid color to accentuate the design.
7. *Layer it.* Create depth, dimension, and visual interest.
8. *Coordinate it.* Layer papers of similar colors and patterns.
9. *Mix it.* Break the rules and combine papers that "clash."
10. *Match it.* Choose papers with the colors of your photos.
11. *Slice it, dice it.* Cut it into strips for borders.
12. *Weave it.* Interlock strips of coordinating papers.
13. *Stretch it.* Use wider strips to create the appearance of an entire background.
14. *Cut it, crop it.* Find a die-cut machine and go to town. Or silhouette-cut printed images.
15. *Carve it.* Cut out lacy designs and lay them over a darker background.
16. *Trim it.* Use all your fancy scissors.
17. *Tear it.* Use the scraps for mosaic designs.
18. *Punch it.* Scraps are perfect for punch art.
19. *Shape it.* Cut a giant heart for a background that fills two pages.
20. *Piece it.* Use remnants to create a quilt background.
21. *Fold it.* Make pockets to keep mementos on a page.
22. *Letter it.* Trace and cut out titles for your pages.
23. *Journal it.* Hand write or use computer fonts on small-patterned papers.
24. *Stamp, stencil, and emboss it.* Great for patterned papers.
25. *Stage it.* Set up photos that will complement your papers.

▲ SPRING HAS SPRUNG, *by Terri Fusco, Alta Loma, CA. Here's a splendid example of what printed papers can do for your scrapbook page. Combining several printed papers with various punches will add pizazz to any page. The patterned flowers and bees are created with punch art, and the green gingham mats visually tie the photos to the grass and leaves.*

Yankee

Doodle

Triston

July 4th 1998   Independence Day   I spent the holiday
playing   at our home in   Naperville, Illinois, with Mommy, Daddy,
twin sister Kathryn, & Auntie Leigh. It was mine & Kathryn's 21 month Birthday.

Oh dear! What is to be the fate of little Kitty Kat!

ROCKET·LAUNCH
★ ★ ★ ★ ★ ★ ★

red of his sisters silly antics, Triston manufactured a rocket of his own design and lured her in..... trapped like a rat! He'll launch it from sea...

◄ *(Previous spread)* Rocket Launch, *by Donna W. Pittard, Kingwood, TX. Donna became a scrapbooker when her twins were born in 1996—now she fills approximately one book for each month of their lives! These July 4th pages are easy, new, and fresh. Using red, white, and blue cardstock, freehand cut shapes for rocket and sailboat. The printed "wave" paper is perfect for the water, and you can almost hear the fireworks that make the sparks of silver and white.*

► Jack O Lantern, *by Dianne Gottron, Hollister, CA. With pumpkin carving and trick-or-treat costumes, Halloween presents some of the best photo opportunities. Everyone loves to see themselves dressed up, or making a mess and having a good time, and Halloween scrapbook pages are often favorites. This page uses colored paper and pens, die cuts, and a kindergarten song for journaling. The children's names are also added to the plain pumpkins.*

You were once a little pumpkin growing on a curly vine. Now you are a Jack O Lantern. Let your candle light SHINE!

SOURCES

Suppliers

Black Ink (303) 442-5499
2300 Central Ave., Suite K
Boulder, CO 80301

C. K. Creations/CK Clips
(888) 451-8080
PO Box 21228
Bradenton, FL 34204

Carl Mfg. 847-956-0730
1862 South Elmhurst Rd.
Mount Prospect, IL 60056
(wholesale only)

Close to My Heart/D.O.T.S.
(888) 655-6552
738 E. Quality Dr.
American Fork, UT 84003

Commotion Rubber Stamps
(800) 225-4894
2711 E Elvira Rd.
Tucson, AZ 85706

Creative Express (800) 468-9335
Coluzzle®
295 W. Center St.
Provo, UT 84601

Creative Memories (800) 563-8679
P.O. Box 1839
St. Cloud, MN 56302-1839

The C-Thru Ruler Co.®
(800) 243-8419
PO Box 356
Bloomfield, CT 06002

Design Originals (800) 877-7820
2425 Cullen St.
Ft. Worth, TX 76107-1411

D.J. Inkers™ (800) 944-4680
PO Box 2462
Sandy, UT 84091

Ellison® Craft & Design
(800) 253-2238
25862 Commercentre Dr.
Lake Forest, CA 92630-8804

Family Treasures, Inc.
(800) 413-2645
24922 Anza Dr., Unit A
Valencia, CA 91355-1229

Fiskars®, Inc. (800) 950-0203
7811 W. Stewart Ave
Wausau, WI 54401

Frances Meyer, Inc.®
(800) 372-6237
PO Box 3088
Savannah, GA 31402

Geographics, Inc.
PO Box 1750
Blaine, WA 98231

The Gifted Line® (800) 533-7263
999 Canal Blvd.
Point Richmond, CA 94804

Hot Off The Press, Inc.®
(800) 227-9595
1250 NW Third Canby, OR 97013

Inspire Graphics (801) 235-9393
PO Box 935
Pleasant Grove, UT 84062

J.D. Impressions (559) 276-1633
PO Box 26895
Fresno, CA 93729-6895

Keeping Memories Alive
(800) 419-4949
PO Box 728
Spanish Fork, UT 84660-0768

Making Memories (800) 286-5263
PO Box 1188
Centerville, UT 84014
(wholesale only)

Mark Enterprises (800) 443-3430
1240 N. Red Gum
Anaheim, CA 92806

Marvy® Uchida (800) 541-5877
3535 Del Amo Blvd.
Torrance, CA 90503

Melissa Neufeld, Inc.
7068 Koll Center Pkwy. Suite 425
Pleasanton, CA 84566

Memory Makers®/Satellite Press
(800) 366-6465
475 W. 115th Ave.
Denver, CO 80234

MPR Associates®, Inc.
(800) 454-3331
PO Box 7343
High Point, NC 27264

Mrs. Grossman's Paper Co.®
(800) 457-4570
3810 Cypress Dr.
Petaluma, CA 94954-5613

The Paper Patch® (800) 397-2737
PO Box 414
Riverton, UT 84065

Pebbles in My Pocket®
(800) 438-8153
PO Box 1506
Orem, UT 84059-1506

Personal Stamp Exchange
(800) 782-6748
360 Sutton Pl.
Santa Rosa, CA 95407

Plaid Enterprises, Inc.
(770) 923-8200
PO Box 7600
Norcross, GA 30091-7600

Provo Craft (800) 937-7686
285 East, 900 South
Provo, UT 84606

SRM Press, Inc. (800) 323-9589
4216 1/2 Glencoe Ave.
Marina del Ray, CA 90292

Sonburn, Inc. (800) 527-7505
PO Box 167
Addison, TX 75001

Stickopotamus® (888) 270-4443
PO Box 1047
Clifton, NJ 07014-1047

West Trim Crafts/Memories
Forever® (818) 998-8550
9667 Canoga Ave.
Chatsworth, CA 91311

page 2
Hugs, Love, and Kisses
Printed paper–The Paper Patch
Rose Stickers–Mrs. Grossman's
Paper Co.

page 9
Daddy's Castle
Cloud paper–Frances Meyer, Inc.
Microtip scissors–Fiskars
Lettering–*Memory Makers*
Nov/Dec., 1998

page 13
Christmas Lights
Bulb clip art–D.J. Inkers

pages 14 and 15
Floral paper–Design Originals
Plaid paper–Sonburn, Inc.
Eliza Jane Originals: Welcome the Seasons–Provo Craft

page 16
Rollin' Rollin' Rollin'
Printed paper–The Paper Patch
"Wow" stickers–Stickopotamus

page 19
Floral Quilt
Printed Papers–Hot Off The Press

page 22
Baby Shower
Umbrella/bear punches–Carl Mfg.
Baby carriage punch–West Trim
Crafts/Memories Forever
Heart and circle stickers–Mrs.
Grossman's Paper Co.

It's Just Intermission
Printed paper–Frances Meyer, Inc.

I Will Give Thanks Sonogram
Gingham paper–Creative
Memories
Plaid paper–Close to My
Heart/D.O.T.S.
Gold star stickers–Mrs.
Grossman's Paper Co.

page 23
Ten Tiny Fingers & Toes
Printed paper–The Paper Patch
Handprint, footprint
stickers–Frances Meyer, Inc.

pages 24–25
Caleb's Bulletin Board
Printed paper–The Paper Patch
Stamps–Close to My
Heart/D.O.T.S

page 29
A Beary Special Girl
Teddy Bear–Creative
Express/Coluzzle
Bear and border stickers–Mrs.
Grossman's Paper Co.

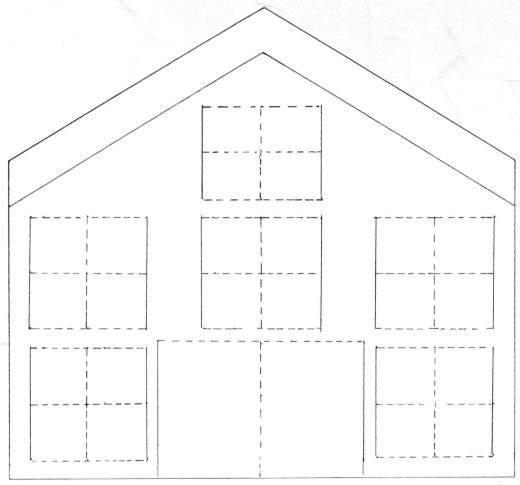

Gingerbread House, pp.104-105

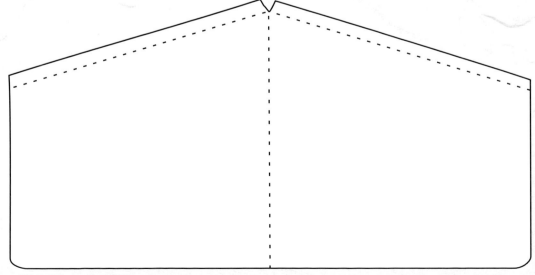

Gloria Pop-up, pp.106-107.

3-D PHOTOS

3-D photos can be created with two copies of the same photo. You carefully cut out the part of the photograph that you want to raise from the page, adhere it to something with a little thickness such as foam core, and place it over the same part of the other photograph copy. See p.38.

JOURNALING

Journaling is just what its name implies, writing the story of your pages in words. Journaling can be as simple as a name and/or date, or it can be a full essay of the event commemorated on your page. It can also be lyrics from a favorite song, or a poem that has special meaning for you. See pp.11, 31.

COLLAGE

Collage is a collection of different photographs pasted together on a page. The elements may or may not overlap. See p.30.

LIFT-THE-FLAPS

Lift-the-flaps pages have windows of paper that you open to reveal a photo or journaling surprise. See p.104.

FOLDED PAPER CUTTING

Folded paper cutting lets you create a perfectly symmetrical design. Fold a piece of scrap paper in half, sketch one half of the design and cut it out. When you unfold the paper, you have a symmetrical template to use on your "real" paper. See p.101.

MATTING

Matting is putting a frame of paper around your photo. You can place the photo onto a piece of paper that is the same shape but slightly larger than the image or make a cutout frame and your photograph behind it. See pp.11, 71.

CROPPING

Cropping means trimming away outside edges of your photos. Cropping is used to get rid of unwanted or unnecessary parts of the photo or to make the photo fit a particular size and shape of space. See pp.11, 38.

MONTAGE

Montage is similar to collage, but the pictures or parts of pictures are superimposed, or overlapped, so that they form a blended whole. See p.109.

EMBOSSING

Embossing involves making a paper design three-dimensional by rubbing it on a raised surface with an embossing stylus, or you can create an embossed image with embossing powder and a heat source (heat gun). See p.86.

MOSAIC

Mosaic is basically the same for the scrapbook artist as the tile artist. You cut photos into small shapes and place them on a page separated by space or a line. Photos could be cut into uniform squares and placed on a page with uniform space around each element. See p.89.

MOUNTING

Mounting simply means applying your photos or other pieces of art to your scrapbook page. See p.11.

PAPER FOLDING

Paper folding is the art of folding paper to create designs. It involves techniques similar to origami and tea-bag folding to produce frames, borders, and embellishments for a scrapbook page. See p.28.

PAPER LAYERING

Paper layering involves cutting out parts of a design to allow a different colored paper to show through. See p.84.

PAPER PIECING

Paper piecing is a technique used to construct a cut paper image from various sources—punches, freehand shapes, or template designs. See p.26.

PAPER PIERCING

Paper piercing is a technique used to accent designs by piercing small holes in the paper. It works particularly well with parchment paper or vellum which allows the under-layering paper to show through. See p.40.

PHOTO KALEIDOSCOPES

Photo kaleidoscopes mimic traditional kaleidoscopes. You cut an equal number of original and reversed image photos into geometric angles and piece them together. See p.46, 81.

POP-UP

Pop-up is the art of cutting, folding and mounting so that when you open a two-page spread a design will "pop up" from the pages. See p.106.

PUNCH ART

Punch art uses any kind of paper punched into a shape with any of the many punches made especially for this purpose. The punched-out shapes may be used as they are or folded and combined with other shapes to create a new image. See p.92.

PUZZLE PAGES

A puzzle page is made by cropping photos into interlocking pieces. A Coluzzle is a template that lets you fit several photos into perfectly interlocking puzzle pieces. Coluzzle designs include a picture frame, rectangle, oval, star, heart, flowerpot, and teddy bear. See p.28.

TEMPLATES

Templates are patterns used as guides in creating a drawn or cut image. See p.35.

MEMORY MAKERS®
FAMILY SCRAPBOOKS
Yesterday, Today & Tomorrow

As Families Gather Memories Grow

Four Generations Reunite to Celebrate Great-Grandma marie's 85TH Birthday

FAMILY
SCRAPBOOKS

MEMORY MAKERS®
FAMILY SCRAPBOOKS
Yesterday, Today & Tomorrow

Michele Gerbrandt with Deborah Cannarella

BEAUX ARTS EDITIONS
IN ASSOCIATION WITH F & W PUBLICATIONS, INC.

Project Director and Editor: Leslie Conron Carola

Design: Kathleen Herlihy-Paoli, Inkstone Design

Copy Editor: Deborah Teipel Zindell

The page ideas features are from the readers and artists of
Memory Makers scrapbook magazine, published by:

F & W Publications, Inc.

4700 East Galbraith Road

Cincinnati, OH 45236

www.memorymakersmagazine.com

FOR MEMORY MAKERS MAGAZINE:

Creative Director: Ron Gerbrandt

Idea Coordinator: Pennie Stutzman

Craft Director: Pam Klassen

Craft Artist: Erikia Ghumm

Photographer: Ken Trujillo

Contributing Photographer: Brenda Martinez

Photo Stylist: Sylvie Abecassis

This book is co-published by Satellite Press and
Hugh Lauter LevinAssociates, Inc.

Printed in China

CONTENTS

....

4TH OF JULY

'97

CREATING A FAMILY SCRAPBOOK

······ ◆ ·····

At first, the task of creating a family scrapbook album may seem a bit overwhelming. There are probably lots of relatives on both sides of your family, some who you yourself don't even know. And there are boxes and boxes of old photos, newspaper clippings, and letters tied in bundles with ribbon, somewhere in your attic. Don't panic. Start small. Begin with the stories of those relatives that you know best. Document the most important events—weddings, anniversaries, birthdays. Then you can expand on any topic or theme that you want—family picnics, the arrival at Ellis Island, opening day of the first family business, long-dreamed-of reunions.

To inspire you, we filled this book with the work of many creative scrapbookers who were inspired to record their family heritage in their own individual ways. And, we also invited colleagues, friends, and family members at Memory Makers to design and create some scrapbook pages—both heritage and contemporary pages—from their own lives, and to work with material contributed by others. In this way we could offer a variety of design possibilities using material from many different sources. You will find pages that are remarkable works of art, complex in scope and presentation—the whole nine yards, as they say— and others that are extremely simple. But all share one element: the pages have been created with a strong sense of the art of presentation.

Some of the scrapbook artists were asked to work with the idea of the family tree—to trace the long family line in a compact and visually appealing way. What a perfect place to start if you're stumped as to how to begin. Find out as much as you can about the relatives that are still living. Tell your aunts, uncles, cousins about your interest in researching the family history. Their stories may surprise you. There are sources at the library and on the Internet to help you research your genealogy. You may also be able to locate a genealogical society in the region where you live. You will want to research your information carefully before recording it, to be sure

◄ 4TH OF JULY, HEATHER MCWHORTER, KOKOMO, INDIANA

·······································

An Independence Day celebration is preserved with small star-cropped photos and tiny stars punched from red, blue, and opalescent stickers exploding from festive fireworks.

► AUTUMN BEAUTY, KAREN KRONE, FLORISSANT, MISSOURI

·······································

Fall photos cut with diamond-shaped templates and arranged into a quilt create a colorful geometric record of a family's visit to Lake of the Ozarks.

that it is accurate. Several software manufacturers have developed computer software that helps you research and record your genealogy on the computer.

FAMILY TREASURES

Sometimes the story begins with an object. Pieces of an old quilt, a Western Union telegram, an ornate silver locket, a lock of hair, a colorful hand-painted trunk. Many of our

▲ SEASONS OF OUR FAMILY, ARTWORK: ERIKIA GHUMM, BRIGHTON, COLORADO, PHOTOS: SHARON DOMINGUEZ, THORNTON, COLORADO

When you research your family tree, start with yourself. A page such as this one with few details allows you to get more creative with the page design, and can prepare you for more extensive family tree pages later on. The photos are simply cropped; the hand-cut leaves supply the journaling platform.

MY GRANDPAS

My Grandpas
and I
We laugh
and play
I'm my
Grandpas' boy
In every
way!

John Patrick Spear Sr. & J.P.

September
7th,
1998

Earl Junior Walker & J.P.

GATHERING INFORMATION FROM FAMILY

Gathering information for your album from older family members can be great fun. We all know that experience is the best teacher, so why not take advantage of the the life experiences of our elders.

• Tape record an interview with your grandparents—hear them talk about their lives in their own words. Have a prepared list of questions for them, but encourage them to add stories as they remember.

• What are their hobbies?

• What are their favorite life moments?

• What were the moments that taught them the most?

• What are the most important life skills?

◄ MY GRANDPAS, KATE SPEAR, CHINO, CALIFORNIA

A simple but special page honoring a newborn boy's two grandfathers. Leaping frogs, baseball bat and ball, a colorful train, and the ultimate toy sports car decorate an all-American-boy page. Double-matted photos on cheerful printed paper in classic red and blue are mounted on a cream background. Names and dates and a short poem are journaled with red ink.

scrapbook artists worked with old photographs, newspaper clippings, and recipe cards as the centerpieces of their pages. Hunt through your own collection of family heirlooms and well-loved objects to see what might inspire you.

Flat objects, like ribbons or buttons, and paper objects, like postcards, photographs, and ticket stubs, can be attached directly onto the page (using acid-free adhesives, of course). Small three-dimensional objects, like jewelry, may also be attached to the pages (using memorabilia boxes or acid-free paper or vellum envelopes). Photograph larger objects—such as furniture, vases, or china, if they are part of your mental image of family— and attach those to your pages. Write about the special meaning of the piece and what you've heard—or still wonder—about it.

Capture the times by putting your ancestors' life stories in the context of the world in which they lived. Consider adding old newspaper clippings of significance, or pages from fashion magazines, or advertisements that tout the newest and latest technology or product. By understanding the everyday events and objects of your ancestors' world, you'll feel closer to them and be better able to relate to them.

Be sure to always use archival materials so as not to damage valuable and precious photographs and heirlooms. With archival papers, inks, and other materials, you will ensure that your family scrapbook will last a long, long time—without suffering deterioration, yellowing, crumbling, or the other effects that scrapbooks suffered in the past.

If you do have any old, crumbling scrapbooks, consider recycling the photographs and stories in them by bringing them to your new scrapbook—giving them a safer and more permanent home.

FAMILY STORIES

We asked some of our scrapbookers to focus their pages on a favorite family story, using photos and journaling to tell a colorful tale that may have been told again and again around the dinner table. Your family's special stories will make your scrapbook pages more personal and more engaging than the typical photo albums that simply show one photo after another. Journal to add information, impressions, and feelings, or provide the context of time and event. Be sure to also include stories about special family traditions, funny or surprising anecdotes, special memories, significant historical events, and even day-to-day realities. Interview your elderly relatives, who still remember what life was like in the good old days, or relatives who live at a distance—as they start to talk, they may even surprise themselves as to the long-forgotten stories and details they begin to remember.

JOURNALING

Journaling—providing written information—is an important component of an interesting scrapbook page. There are as many ways to journal as there are to crop your photos. The journaling can be minimal, simple identification, or it can be the main event. That depends on the purpose and style of your pages. The simple handwritten letter of affection for a favorite family member—Morgan, the Irish setter—is one style, direct and clean. You can add color and drama to your heavily journaled pages by emphasizing individual words the way you do in conversation.

▶ MY BIRTHDAY, ARTWORK: PAM KLASSEN, WESTMINSTER, COLORADO, PHOTO: JULIE LABUSZEWSKI, LITTLETON, COLORADO

Tiny illustrations woven into the text, and certain words made bigger and bolder for emphasis are visually commanding.

◀ MY DARLING MORGAN, SANDRA DE ST. CROIX, ST. ALBERT, ALBERTA, CANADA

A long letter from a pet owner to her dog, Morgan, with simple decorations and two photos tell him just how much he is loved. The simple, direct page has a place of honor in a family scrapbook.

◀ REBUS DISNEY SCRAPBOOK, KRISTY HAMILTON, FAIRFAX, VIRGINIA

Rebus journaling is a fun way to present a story and is almost sure to engage young readers—and writers—with the use of small illustrations that substitute for words. These Disney vacation pages literally come alive with the sights of Sea World. Plan your rebus pages carefully so you don't run out of space. Every word—and picture word—is equally important and you want to be sure to have plenty of room to tell your story.

They came by Tall Ship to

The Sydney 2000 Olympics have just finished, and even little Beth, a 2, has learnt to chant 'Aussie Aussie Aussie Oi Oi Oi!' whilst waving our flag. Rory, at 4½, has just worked out that he really is an Australian (he sort of thought he might be Canadian!) So I thought I should take my 'mum duties' a bit more seriously and tell them how they came to be Australian in the first place. So, Rory and Beth... this little story is for you: The first Australians were the aboriginal people. They have lived here al for ever, but white people like us haven't. Australia is a huge island surrounded by water, and the only way to get here used be by sailing ship. These pictures are of an old sailing ship called the 'Polly Woodside'. You thought it was a pirate ship because it had lots of piratey things, like big white sails, a crow's nest, rigging, a big wheel to steer with...but no cannon treasure chests (we looked!) Do you remember how old it seer The wind was rustling the sails, and the wooden masts and si of the ship creaked all the time. A sailor was climbing the ma und working in the rigging. Seagulls were screeching for foo and waves were swashing against the sides. Beth was really scared of the dark when we went down the ladder, and the cabins where the crew lived were really tiny with little bunks or swinging hammocks to sleep in. There was no electricity, so the were lit by candles. Do you remember the handrail outside t galley (the ship's kitchen) where you thought the pirates hung t towels to dry? Now - close your eyes, and see if you can use your wonderful imagination to bring that ship alive... because.... Once upon a time, a long, long tim ago, when pirates really DID exist, people in your own family (who are called your ancestors) sailed on ships a lot like this to come all the way from Britain to Australia. Your first ancesto to come here arrived with the very first fleet, in 1788. Aeroplanes had not even been dreamed of y so this was the only way to travel. Ships were pushed along by the wind (motors hadn't been invented), so the trip took many, many months. Can you imagine living on a boat like that sleeping and eating with more than 100 people in that tiny space, from Easter to Christmas? Tha was about 240 sleeps! Think of all those people talking and fighting, and being seasick, and th awful smell because they couldn't wash very often except in a bucket of sea water. There wer such things as showers or flush toilets then – yuck! The food was horrible too, because there were

▲ TALL SHIP TO AUSTRALIA, HELEN SHIPPERLEE, THORNBURY, VICTORIA, AUSTRALIA

This scrapbook artist accepted the challenge to tell a favorite family story in an extraordinary way. A young mother tells her two young children about an ancestor's hard journey by sea from Ireland to Australia. The sea-blue palette provides the perfect background for the family story written in soft colors against a midnight blue sea. The story is brought up to the present with images of the youngsters touring a tall ship. One can tell a story to a child, but presenting that story with visual excitement is a gift for generations. What a lovely way to remember who you are and where you came from.

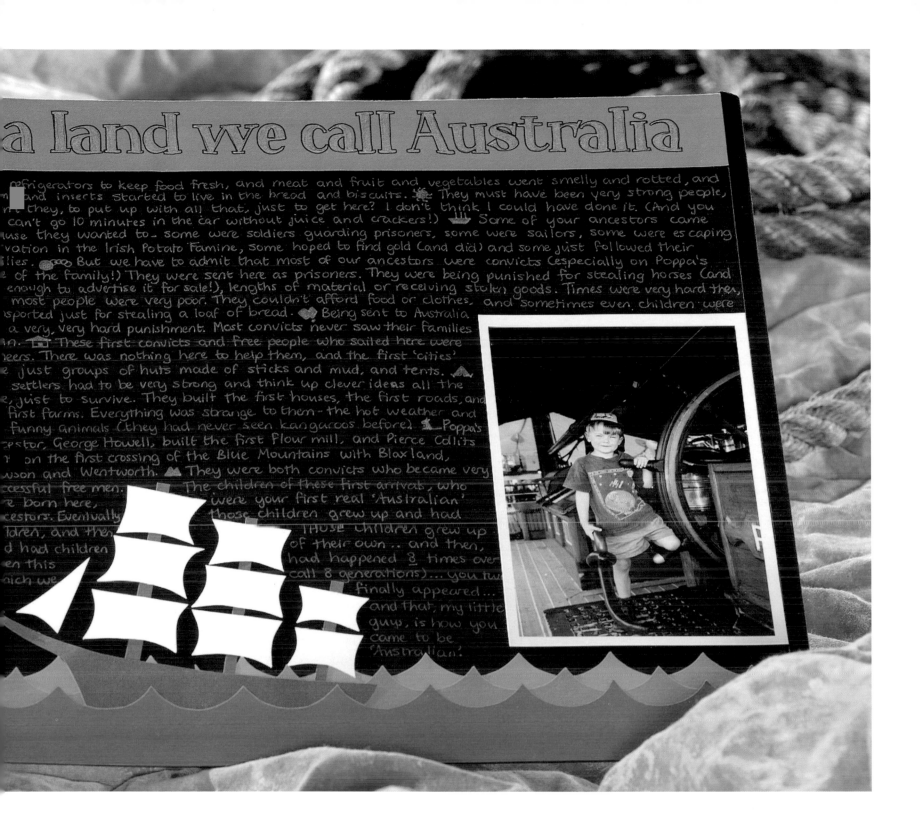

a land we call Australia

...frigerators to keep food fresh, and meat and fruit and vegetables went smelly and rotted, and ...and insects started to live in the bread and biscuits. They must have been very strong people, ...n't they, to put up with all that, just to get here? I don't think I could have done it. (And you can't go 10 minutes in the car without juice and crackers!) Some of your ancestors came ...use they wanted to - some were soldiers guarding prisoners, some were sailors, some were escaping ...vation in the Irish Potato Famine, some hoped to find gold (and did) and some just followed their ...lies. But we have to admit that most of our ancestors were convicts (especially on Poppa's ...e of the family!) They were sent here as prisoners. They were being punished for stealing horses (and ...enough to advertise it for sale!), lengths of material or receiving stolen goods. Times were very hard then, ...most people were very poor. They couldn't afford food or clothes, and sometimes even children were ...sported just for stealing a loaf of bread. Being sent to Australia ...a very, very hard punishment. Most convicts never saw their families ...n. These first convicts and free people who sailed here were ...eers. There was nothing here to help them, and the first 'cities' ...e just groups of huts made of sticks and mud, and tents. ...settlers had to be very strong and think up clever ideas all the ...e, just to survive. They built the first houses, the first roads, and ...first farms. Everything was strange to them - the hot weather and ...funny animals (they had never seen kangaroos before). Poppa's ...estor, George Howell, built the first flour mill, and Pierce Collits ...t on the first crossing of the Blue Mountains with Blaxland, ...wson and Wentworth. They were both convicts who became very ...cessful free men. The children of these first arrivals, who ...e born here, were your first real 'Australian' ...cestors. Eventually those children grew up and had ...ldren, and then those children grew up ...d had children of their own .. and then, ...en this had happened 8 times over ...ich we call 8 generations)... you tw... finally appeared ... and that, my little guy, is how you came to be 'Australian'.

▲ AS FAMILIES GATHER, ARTWORK: ERIKIA GHUMM, BRIGHTON, COLORADO, AND PAM KLASSEN, WESTMINSTER, COLORADO, PHOTO: GERALD TRAFFICANDA

A birthday party California style for Great-Grandma Marie. The simple family photo is treated to two presentations. Both pages are filled with colored and printed papers, stamped and die-cut images, and lots of layers and texture.

DESIGN

When you begin to think about actually putting your project on paper it's time to think about how it will look. What is the purpose of the page? Do you want the photos themselves to tell the story, or is the journaling meant to tell it and the photos serve as illustrations? Both are powerful. How many images do you want to include on the page? Is one more dominant than another? Are you going to mat the photos, frame them, decorate them? What color scheme will work best?

We decided to present two different color treatments for the same scrapbook page to show the effect of color. Look at the two pages above and decide which you like best. Soft, muted violets, greens, and creams are lovely and provide a quiet background for a lively colored photo of a family gathering. A more dramatic palette of contrasting colors makes a strong statement. The bright colors *frame* the central photo; the softer colors *present* the central photo. On the page opposite one simple punched design frame created in three different color schemes offers completely different effects and elicits totally different responses from the viewer.

In addition to color, you will want to think about texture and layering. What kind of special effects will you use? What technique—quilting, quilling, pierced paper, torn paper, punching, stamping, a single photo, several photos, etc. This is a time to have fun, to experiment, to be creative.

▲ DUTCH ART FRAMES, ARTWORK: PAM METZGER, BOULDER, COLORADO

It's great fun to work with punches. Here we have used a few simple shapes sparingly to provide charming frames for three quite different traditional photographs.

(ABOVE LEFT) Bright, primary hues command a sense of elementary fun! (Photo: Megan Brockbank, San Diego, California)

(ABOVE CENTER) Two shades of blue give the punched shape a cool, monochromatic feel. (Photo: Karen Gerbrandt, Broomfield, Colorado)

(ABOVE RIGHT) Deep red, black, burnt umbers, and goldenrod lend a timeless, classic touch.

◄ TYLER AND MARCI, NANCY SCHROEDER, YORK, MAINE

Once again we see the powerful effectiveness of one simple central photograph surrounded by simple decorations. In this case the fern-like green leaves are touched up with a black pen, the tan flower-petal decorated background paper supports the lush flowers in the featured image, and the gorgeous pink hydrangea is a perfect finishing touch.

▲ GENERATIONS OF FAMILY, CHERYL THOMAS, HIGHLAND, CALIFORNIA

Here, a well-thought-out and beautifully executed scrapbook page of a family tree demonstrates the artist's perceptive sense of color and texture. The leaves punched from soft, unusual "leaf" colors cascade very dramatically against the dark background. The bark-like crinkled, layered paper of the trunk and branches adds texture and depth to the page. Craft wire adds to the texture. Mats cut with decorative-edged scissors present the simply cropped images without fanfare. Minimal, attractive, handwritten journaling completes the page. The photos are simple, the presentation stunning.

Yassky Family
Passage from Russia

The Yassky family migrated from Belarouse, Russia because they were persecuted for their religious beliefs. Many years later their Great Great Grandson ran for office and got to meet President Clinton.

In America, the Yasskys were free to celebrate religious traditions, such as a barmitzvah, from the 1950's.

1998 looking back at their success during a Yassky family reunion.

AN AMERICAN DREAM

Dreams can be short term or long term. This page celebrates and rejoices in the good lives of an American family. Not too long ago— just a few generations, in fact— the forbears of the handsome young politician seen shaking hands with President Clinton in the White House emigrated from Russia in search of a better life in the United States.

—*Artwork: Erikia Ghumm, Brighton, Colorado, Photos: Ellin Yassky*

YOU'RE

BLAKES

TEA

PARTY

BIRTHDAY
5·8·99

FIVE

GARRETT'S

OUR

1997

FEB. 28

SON

1ST YEAR

A MERRY

GARRETT
&
DALTON

BARBRA
&
LORA

MICHELLE

KAYLA

1998

CONNOR
&

BLAKE

CHRISTMAS

WORKING WITH TEMPLATES

We have included in this book many different techniques from the past to demonstrate both diversity and continuity. Quilting and scrapbooking have much in common. And scrapbookers love to adapt other craft techniques to their own. The technique is basically the same. What is most exciting to scrapbookers is that each quilt pattern can be adapted to complement the photos. Changing the color of the pattern can make it fit your photo and/or color scheme. The patterns themselves are largely composed of various geometric shapes arranged in countless appealing ways. Quilters rarely work without the help of templates —they help to give patterns their crisp, clean, uniform shapes and edges. Templates are just one of the many tools that scrapbookers have borrowed from these fabric artists.

POSITIVE TEMPLATES—To work with positive templates, simply place the template on your paper and trace around the outside edges. Next, cut along the line you've drawn. Because you can't see through these templates, it is easiest to use them on solid colored paper. They may be difficult to place perfectly on a patterned sheet.

NEGATIVE TEMPLATES—A negative template is usually made of paper or plastic, and the interior of the template shape is cut out. With this type of template, you can see exactly what your shaped image will look like after you cut it. Negative templates are great for cropping photos or for selecting a specific pattern in a printed paper. Move the template around until it is positioned over just the section of the photo or paper that you want. Trace the interior edges of the shape, and then cut your photo or paper to its finished size.

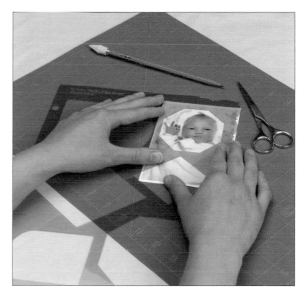

MAKE YOUR OWN TEMPLATES—Quilting books are full of patterns that scrapbookers can use to make templates. You'll need tracing paper and a light board. Trace around the quilting template and cut out the shape. Now, trace this pattern onto cardboard or other sturdy stock or onto stencil film (if you want a see-through template). Decide whether you want a negative or positive template. If you want a positive template, cut along the outline of the shape. If you want a negative template, cut out the interior of the shape.

Photos: Debra Fee, Broomfield, Colorado

◀ AUNT ELIZA'S STAR, ARTWORK: ERIKIA GHUMM, BRIGHTON, COLORADO, PHOTO: LORA MASON, WINTER PARK, FLORIDA

Aunt Eliza's star pattern works for three very different-looking pages. Varying the color schemes and the patterned papers complements the colors in the photographs—birthday, Christmas, and baby's first year.

September 7, 1968

<KATHLEEN
PAULA KENNEDY,
AMANDA WILSON,
COLORADO SPRINGS,
COLORADO

Every wedding photo is a one-of-a-kind, and this lovely bride's classic origami frame encircles this memorable portrait in a stunning wreath. Beautiful papers folded and assembled together add a third-dimensional richness to an already important photo.

Kathleen Paula Kennedy

PAPER FOLDING

What more perfect complement to your paper scrapbook page than embellishments made of folded paper? With just a few folds and creases, a two-dimensional composition becomes a strong three-dimensional statement. The "kite" fold explained below is the basic form for the wreath that Amanda Wilson, of Colorado Springs, Colorado, created to frame this beautiful formal bridal portrait. The composition may look complicated, but it is simply sixteen folded squares layered in a circle.

To assemble the wreath, hold two finished pieces with closed points facing the same direction, then slide one piece into the space between the kite and flap of the other piece. Position the pieces so that the closed point of the inserted kite covers half of the wing of the other piece. Layer the folds around the circle. For this page, layer the kite folds around a 4 1/2-inch circle.

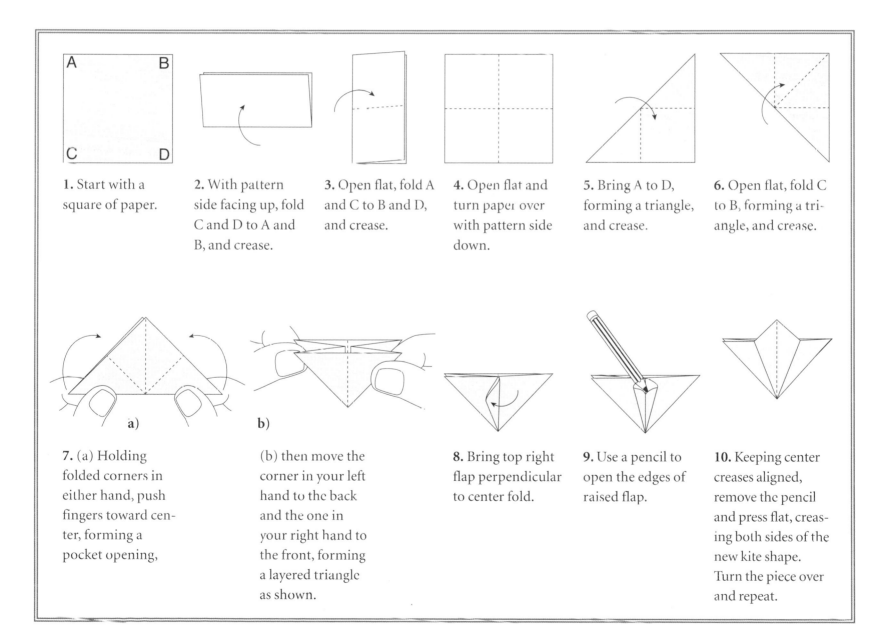

1. Start with a square of paper.

2. With pattern side facing up, fold C and D to A and B, and crease.

3. Open flat, fold A and C to B and D, and crease.

4. Open flat and turn paper over with pattern side down.

5. Bring A to D, forming a triangle, and crease.

6. Open flat, fold C to B, forming a triangle, and crease.

a)

b)

7. (a) Holding folded corners in either hand, push fingers toward center, forming a pocket opening,

(b) then move the corner in your left hand to the back and the one in your right hand to the front, forming a layered triangle as shown.

8. Bring top right flap perpendicular to center fold.

9. Use a pencil to open the edges of raised flap.

10. Keeping center creases aligned, remove the pencil and press flat, creasing both sides of the new kite shape. Turn the piece over and repeat.

◀ MOM AND HER FRIEND CHERYL, ARTWORK: PAM KLASSEN, WESTMINSTER, COLORADO, PHOTO: JOYCE HANSEN, LITTLETON, COLORADO

Working with vellum offers many ways to add an elegant or whimsical finishing touch to your project. Here, torn layers of colored and patterned vellum fill out the chorus. The treatment is fun-loving and upbeat.

▶ CHILI BABY, REBECCA HANSON, GILBERT, ARIZONA

Rebecca took several photos of her daughter wearing a chili pepper costume and then silhouetted the photos and gathered them together to make a strand of chilis. The knot at the top of the chili pepper strand is cut from tan paper.

▲ MOM'S WEDDING, LINDA STRAUSS, PROVO, UTAH

Handmade, rose-strewn paper provides the support for this timeless photograph of young bride and attendant. The soft paper corners gently lift the photo off the page.

▲ OUR FAMILY CHRISTMAS 1997, ARTWORK: ERIKIA GHUMM, BRIGHTON, COLORADO, PHOTOS: SANDRA ESCOBEDO, MANTECA, CALIFORNIA

A solid green tree and festive gifts under the tree are festooned with cut strips of patterned vellum in several colors. A paper crimper gives texture to the vellum. Freehand cut stars and hearts, also of patterned vellum, complete the family holiday picture.

MY WEDDING SHOWER, ANNETTE GRYMONPRE, TALLAHASSEE, FLORIDA

When creating a scrapbook for her wedding shower, the bride-to-be selected a favorite appliqué quilt motif. This creative and complex-looking title page is made up of only four shapes—a leaf, flower, heart, and circle. The umbrella in the center reinforces the scrapbook theme. The hearts are punched. The page is also accented with a mat cut with fancy scissors. Stylized images and a bold heading contribute to a strong graphic presentation.

HEART QUILT, MARILYN GARNER, SAN DIEGO, CALIFORNIA

A scrapbook page with definite attitude, embracing three passions: family, quilting, and scrapbooking itself. The charming photos cropped and matted to fit inside the appliqué flower shapes and arranged in a heart shape let you know this is a well-loved family.

OUR FAMILY, MARTY MUELLER, EDEN PRAIRIE, MINNESOTA

A title page adds a special finishing touch to your scrapbook. Add journaling of names and dates or meaningful verses to make your scrapbook uniquely your own. The images for this page were created with punches on a precut laser die-cut mat and then assembled into a striking wreath. The beautifully handwritten poem (author unknown) describes the essence of family.

*The inspiration for this timeline
that records the life of this
scrapbooker's father—from
babyhood to parenthood—
came from the classic board
game, "Game of Life." A game-
board created from brightly colored cut paper provides the base
for wonderful photos cropped
and layered on its route.
Stickers and simple journaling
bring the board to life.*

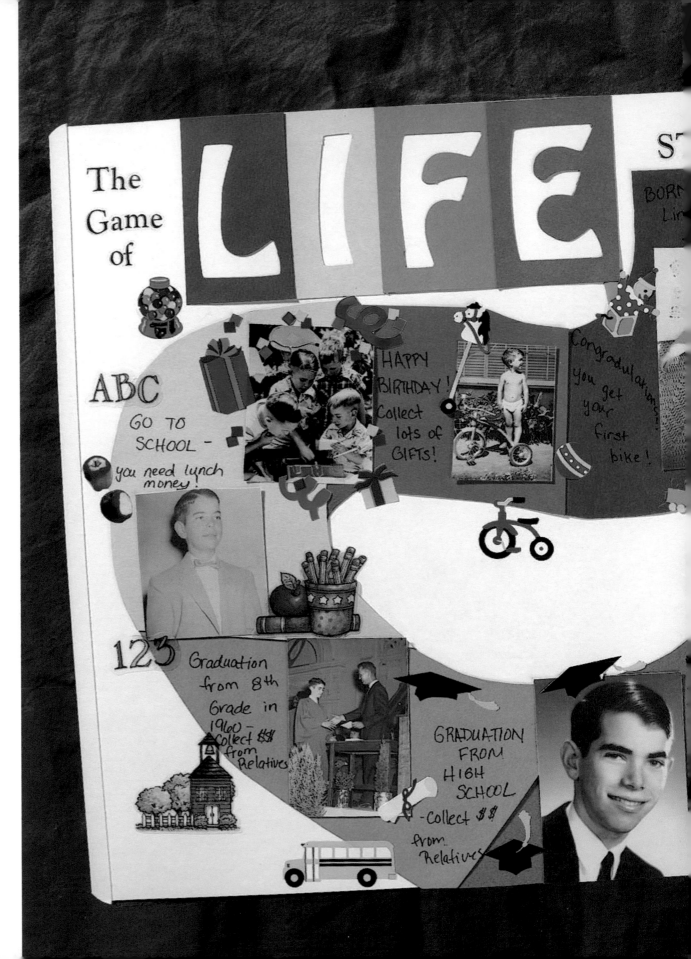

Get Married
June 28, 1969

Buy a house in Jacksonville, FL
2445 Patsy Anne Dr.

Get Engaged
December 1968

Pay for the wedding

Buy an engagement ring

Joanna Leigh
April 20, 1973

Induction into the Navy 1968

Get military pay #

Late 1973
Steve was Diagnosed with Multiple Sclerosis

Your first daughter is born - Buy lots of Diapers

RX

She has Cancer Go to Hospital Pay Bills

ouch!

Jennifer Lynn
July 4, 1974
Your 2nd daughter is born

Class Notes

ego State

Hyrum and Maria Jensen Olsen - Wedding Day
LDS Logan Temple, Utah - March 6, 1895

YESTERDAY: CELEBRATING YOUR HERITAGE

As we travel from yesterday into tomorrow, from generation to generation, our scrapbooks tell the stories of our lives. With pictures and words, we record our fondest memories and celebrate our connection to the past. Scrapbooks inspire us to reach across time, to rediscover our heritage and our traditions, and to retell our most treasured family stories.

The pages of your scrapbook capture the spirit, faces, and voices of your ancestors—whether they lived long ago or in the recent past. With a little creativity and some of the objects that you have tucked away through the years—portraits, old letters, bits of heirloom lace—you can bring your family's story to life. Create a family tree, journal the funny stories Grandma used to tell you, interview Uncle Lou about what life was like when he was a boy.

Preserve all the memories that matter to you most. The story you tell will be as unique as the people who lived it. What will make your book special to future generations are those small details—the little-known facts about family and friends, the heartfelt traditions, the festive holiday events, and the favorite stories that make these people and places live in your memory. As you build your scrapbook, you'll feel the sense of your own identity deepen—as an individual and as part of a family. You'll develop a new sense of pride in your heritage as you create a strong bond with the past and tie to the future.

◄ HYRUM AND MARIA,
LAURIE NELSON CAPENER,
PROVIDENCE, UTAH

With touches of gold against a monochromatic color scheme, this heritage wedding page emphasizes the dignity of this couple and their solemn intent. The laser die-cut mat adds an additional touch of Old World elegance.

▲ SIX GENERATIONS, NICOLE RAMSAROOP, HORST, THE NETHERLANDS

Nicole made this heritage quilt page for her daughter. She collected the old photographs from her great-aunt in Holland—the oldest living member of her family.

The past gives shape to our lives today. It is also the foundation on which the next generations build their future. What better place to begin a family scrapbook than with the stories of the people that came before us? As the older members of the family grow older, we realize the importance of preserving their stories and memories. How many times the world over have children begged "Tell me a story, Grandpa, tell me about 'the olden days'?" Take that opportunity now and present those stories in your own visually meaningful way.

FAMILY TREE, ARTWORK: ERIKIA GHUMM, BRIGHTON, COLORADO; PHOTOS: MARY ANNE DENNEY, LAKEWOOD, COLORADO

Make a family tree to record the names, dates, and places of birth, death, and marriage of relatives. You can fill the "branches" in many imaginative ways. Family lines are usually quite long. The "leaves" of this handcut-paper tree present a lot of information in an appealing and space-efficient way.

▲ ROOTS AND BRANCHES, JOY CAREY, VISALIA, CALIFORNIA

To make it easy to update her computer-generated genealogies, this scrapbooker mounts the page with clear photo mounts. When she wants to update her information, she simply removes the old page and inserts the new one. The printed page is matted on dark green paper, which is mounted on a pale green parchment background.

◄ FAMILY TREE, LISA JACKSON, SAN ANTONIO, TEXAS

This family tree is just one page in an entire album created as a remembrance of Lisa's grandmother's 100th birthday celebration. Leaf die cuts, photos, ribbon, and rose stickers make a brightly colored tree that blooms with the memory of loved ones.

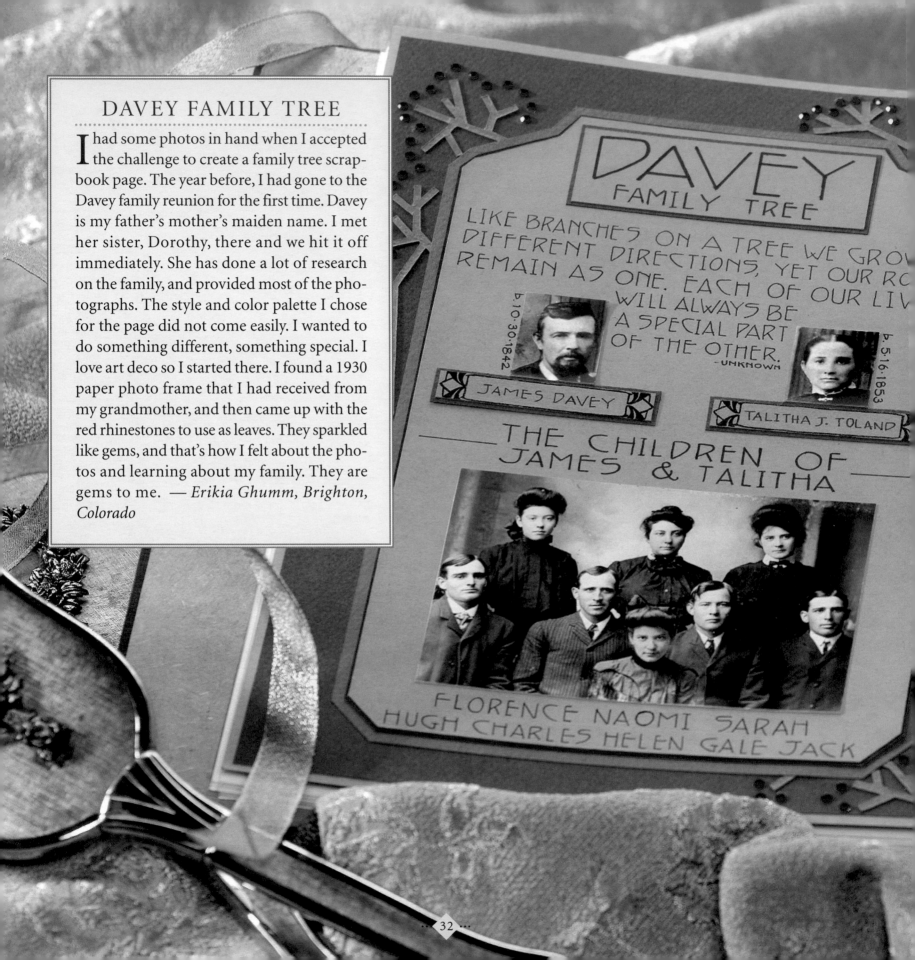

DAVEY FAMILY TREE

I had some photos in hand when I accepted the challenge to create a family tree scrapbook page. The year before, I had gone to the Davey family reunion for the first time. Davey is my father's mother's maiden name. I met her sister, Dorothy, there and we hit it off immediately. She has done a lot of research on the family, and provided most of the photographs. The style and color palette I chose for the page did not come easily. I wanted to do something different, something special. I love art deco so I started there. I found a 1930 paper photo frame that I had received from my grandmother, and then came up with the red rhinestones to use as leaves. They sparkled like gems, and that's how I felt about the photos and learning about my family. They are gems to me. — *Erikia Ghumm, Brighton, Colorado*

DAVEY FAMILY TREE

LIKE BRANCHES ON A TREE WE GROW DIFFERENT DIRECTIONS, YET OUR RO REMAIN AS ONE. EACH OF OUR LIV WILL ALWAYS BE A SPECIAL PART OF THE OTHER. —UNKNOWN

b.10-30-1842

JAMES DAVEY

b.5-16-1853

TALITHA J. TOLAND

THE CHILDREN OF JAMES & TALITHA

FLORENCE NAOMI SARAH
HUGH CHARLES HELEN GALE JACK

b.1·20·1875 **W. GALE DAVEY**

b.11·11·1888 **HILDEGARDE A. POULSEN**

THE CHILDREN OF GALE & HILDEGARD

b.5·31·1910

A. FERN DAVEY

b.12·20·1925 **W. GALE DAVEY JR.**

b.2·22·1917 **DOROTHY D. DAVEY**

b.10·3·1922 **ALBERT A. DAVEY**

b.1·23·1913 **ROSE L. DAVEY**

b.1·16·1915 **CHARLES J. DAVEY**

b.3·25·1908 **R. EUGENE DAVEY**

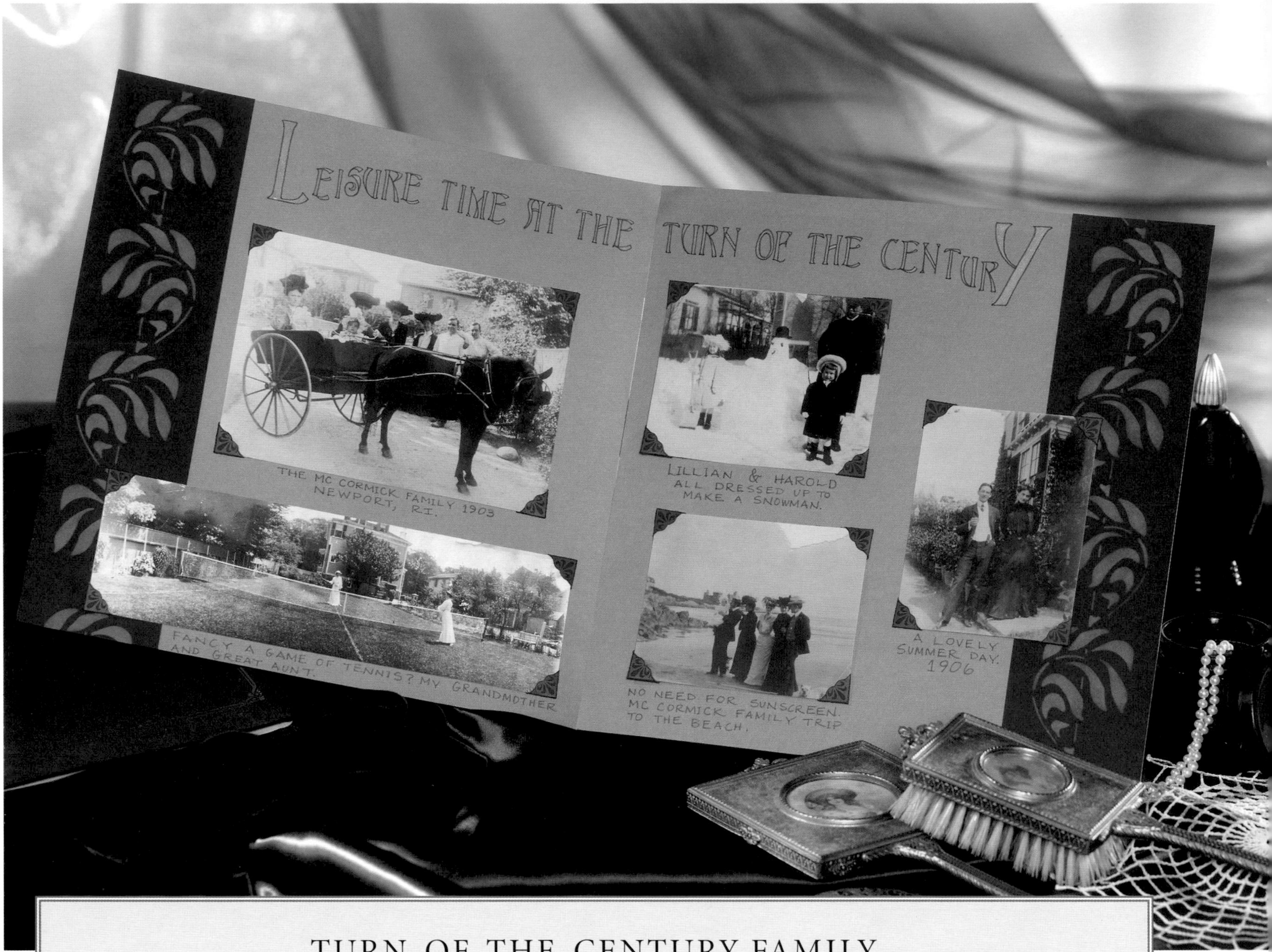
LEISURE TIME AT THE TURN OF THE CENTURY
THE MC CORMICK FAMILY 1903 NEWPORT, R.I.
LILLIAN & HAROLD ALL DRESSED UP TO MAKE A SNOWMAN.
A LOVELY SUMMER DAY. 1906
FANCY A GAME OF TENNIS? MY GRANDMOTHER AND GREAT AUNT.
NO NEED FOR SUNSCREEN. MC CORMICK FAMILY TRIP TO THE BEACH.

TURN-OF-THE-CENTURY FAMILY

When my mother died a few years ago, her twin sister, the only remaining sibling of their family of five, brought down from her attic several boxes of old family photos and asked if I'd like to go through them while she could still identify everyone! Some of the people I knew, some I didn't, some had died before I was born. The feelings emanating from the photos were warm and congenial, and quietly celebratory. My aunt's lovely smile widened as she remembered the moments: children showing off their just-created snowman to their father; grandmother taking some children for a ride in a jaunty horse and buggy; an adults' winter Sunday afternoon walk on the beach carrying an adored first child; a tennis game at home; Aunt Lilly, coquettish, with a "beau." What a treat. *—Ellen Brunelle, artwork: Erikia Ghumm, Brighton, Colorado*

MY GRANDFATHER, WILLIAM MAHER

I tracked down a journal I had heard of that had been written by a great-grandfather, born in 1840 in Quebec, Canada. "My Journal and History of My Life," it read, "the Days of My Childhood, the Rambles and Pleasures of My Boyhood Days, the Death of My Parents, My Departure from Home, My Travels through Canada and the United States, and Three Years in the Army." Begun in 1866, the worn, yellowed pages in rather arch handwriting read like a nineteenth-century novel: large happy family, parents die young, children separated, walking from Quebec to Chicago at the age of fourteen, finding work, joining the Army, etc. I don't even remember having seen a photograph of him before. Reading his journal made him come alive. The journal itself was incomplete; it just trailed off as he went to fight in the Civil War. At the end, though, were some pages with a price list of plants that he, then a landscape gardener and florist, offered for sale in the spring of 1875. It was like a door opening. The plant list today is very much the same, though the prices differ slightly.

—*Maria Barry, artwork: Erikia Ghumm, Brighton, Colorado*

QUILTING

LAZY DAISY QUILT PATTERN

One of the nicest aspects of scrapbooking is the opportunity it presents to include ideas and techniques from other crafts. Quilting has always been an important craft and quilt patterns are a popular motif with scrapbookers. Quilt patterns can be adapted to create beautiful borders, frames, or even the central motif on a large page.

This Lazy Daisy quilt-style page combines a patchwork motif and a distinctive style of raised "stitching" called trapunto. The star and chevron patches are made with diamonds cut from red and blue cardstock. The "stitching" pattern is made by tracing a feather pattern on a lightbox.

1. Using the chevron template on page 140, enlarge if necessary, trace, and cut out twenty-four red and twenty-four blue cardboard diamonds.

2. Carefully cut the diamonds out. Be accurate; the diamonds need to fit together neatly to form a star, but if they don't, you can trim them later.

3. Crop your photo to a round shape with a template, about $3^1/2$ inches in diameter. Find the center of your scrapbook page by drawing diagonals from corner to corner lightly with a pencil and ruler. Center the photo on the page.

Assemble the stars in each of the corners, carefully placing diamonds of alternating colors to make the shape. Next, make two chevrons between each star to form the border.

To create the effect of raised trapunto stitching, use a lightbox and a light tan pen to trace the feather pattern around the center photo. "Stitch" a crosshatch pattern in the squares in the border with the same pen. Add shadowing within the feather pattern using tan chalk and a cotton swab.

With a pen, add "stitching" lines around the inside edges of the red and blue diamonds. Add a title or journaling to the page.

▶ THE BEAR FAMILY 1897, JOY CAREY, VISALIA, CALIFORNIA

A descendant of the Bear family combined quilting traditions of the mid-nineteenth century—the Lazy Daisy patchwork pattern and trapunto stitching, a raised design technique—to create this frame for a vintage family portrait.

The Bear Family

1897

LOG CABIN QUILT PATTERN

The logic and format of quilting lends itself readily to scrapbookers. What you can do with fabric you can do with paper. We feature adaptations of three distinctive quilt patterns in this book, showing the variety of treatments that are possible in the creation of your scrapbook pages. And somehow, that connection to the past—to the past of quilters—adds a further dimension to the creation of our own scrapbook pages.

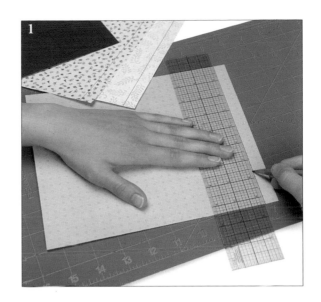

Four Log Cabin quilt blocks serve as the background for the photograph of—naturally—lumberjacks! The basic block of this design is called the Spiraling Log Cabin. To create shading, dark-print papers are used on one half of the block, and light-print papers on the other.

1. Choose a variety of light and dark printed papers. Use a ruler and pencil to mark thirty-two strips, ¹/₂ inch wide, on the light-print paper and thirty-two strips of the same width on the dark-print paper.

2. Cut out the strips with a scissors or use the ruler and a craft knife to cut the strips on a flat, protected surface. Divide your scrapbook page into quarters, drawing lines with the ruler and pencil.

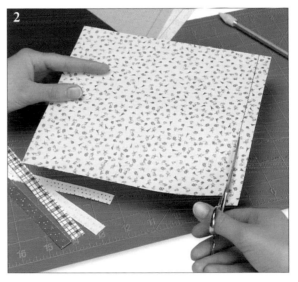

3. Work with the template on page 140 to create a block in each quarter of the page. Dark strips are positioned in the shaded areas and light strips in the unshaded areas. Glue down the light strips first, working from the center of the page. Finish one block before starting the next.

When the blocks are finished, glue a 2-inch red square at the center of each one. Crop and double-mat your photograph with black and white papers. Make the mats very narrow so they don't hide too much of the quilt background. Add journaling to the red squares at the center of the blocks.

◄ SPIRALING LOG CABIN, DEBRA FEE, BROOMFIELD, COLORADO

Using strips of various colored printed paper, the Log Cabin pattern is a popular design for quilters and scrapbookers alike. The pattern begins with one square in the center around which strips or long, narrow rectangles are arranged. Frequently, as with this page, the Log Cabin quilts featured a red square in the center to symbolize the hearth as the center of the home. The structure of the four basic tan, black, red, and white pieced blocks supports a wonderful black-and-white photograph of two hardworking lumberjacks.

In October 1917 Peter Thiessen was a widower. He ha[s]
nine children and twenty seven grand children.

▲ PETER THIESSEN FAMILY 1917, ARTWORK: ERIKIA GHUMM, BRIGHTON, COLORADO, PHOTOS: ALMA FRANZ,
INMAN, KANSAS

Studio group portraits with their warm and inviting colors invoke sweet memories of bygone days. Here a simple classic proscenium frames the formal family portrait in muted colors. Journaling along the bottom of the page names the widower Peter Thiessen—father of nine and grandfather of twenty-seven.

CREATING YOUR FAMILY ARCHIVES

Begin your research by contacting as many relatives as you can and telling them about your interest. Everyone has his or her own story, and the more relatives you find, the more history you'll uncover.

Obtain and begin to fill out ancestor charts or family group charts. You can find these basic forms in books, at genealogy societies, and library genealogy departments. Or start with a simple list. Begin with yourself and work back generation by generation, filling in names and dates for each family member as you gather the information.

Be sure you can verify the information you collect. Don't overlook the official documents you may already have at home—certificates of birth, marriage, and death—and the more informal records, such as report cards, family Bibles, obituaries in newspapers, wedding programs, and so on. Ask your relatives to do the same. It's a good idea to transcribe any audio or videotaped interviews since these tapes have limited lifespans. Any information you are missing may be on record in local county offices—real estate deeds, wills, military pensions, for example.

Find out about genealogy at the library and contact local genealogical societies in your area. The research process can be overwhelming, and the support of others with similar interests can be very helpful.

Respect the privacy of the living. You may well come upon family problems or colorful facts about your ancestors that would be hurtful to some living relatives if uncovered. And don't give out too many details on Web sites. The whereabouts of some family members might best not be made public for various reasons.

DIGITAL RESTORATION

Digital restoration is one way to preserve old photographs—without their imperfections! A professional photo finisher can scan the photo, repair any visible tears or discoloration, and print out the image at whatever size you need for your scrapbook page. To make sure you always have a copy of the photograph, ask the photo lab to store the corrected image for you on a disc. Store the disc at home in a safe place.

WORKING WITH HISTORIC PHOTOS

For an archival-quality album environment:
- *Assume all memorabilia is acidic; never let photos and memorabilia touch.*
- *Use only acid- and lignin-free papers, photo-safe adhesives, and pigment inks.*
- *Handle photos with care, avoiding direct light.*
- *Use nonpermanent mounting techniques (photo corners, sleeves, etc.) for easy removal for copying or restoration.*
- *Keep cropping to a minimum; background objects tell their own stories of place and time.*
- *Don't trim or hand tint old photos; have reprints made first.*

Artwork: Debbie Mock, Littleton, Colorado

Several times each summer either prairie hay or alfalfa is cut with a horse-drawn mower and left to dry on the ground.

Then it is raked into piles with a horse-drawn dump rake. Each time you lift the lever to dump a load you get a hit on the seat.

These piles are then picked up with an implement called a go-devil. When it is full it is lifted slightly, brought to the stack and then dumped.

These stacks are feed for the livestock in the winter months when pastures are dry. These photos date back to 1909.

▲ HAYING TIME, ARTWORK: ERIKIA GHUMM, BRIGHTON, COLORADO, PHOTOS: ALMA FRANZ, INMAN, KANSAS

Erikia was given the photos and story for this page. The photos themselves actually tell the story of harvest time, summer 1909, on a Kansas farm. A dark green barn-siding background sets the stage for the series of photos bordered with black marker and the starkly simple wagon wheel. The earth-toned straightforward presentation reflects the strength of the hard-working men. Hand-cut paper elements reflect the time when things were hand made.

DADDY & FRIENDS
Joy Riding
UNCLE JAKE DADDY AND FRIENDS SLEDDING.
DADDY ATTENDED TABOR COLLEGE IN HILLSBORO, KANSAS. 1912
DADDY AND HIS COUSIN JOHN KROEKER. 1910
After Blizzard Feb. 27 - 12
I.C.S. REFERENCE LIBRARY

DADDY AND FRIENDS

College men enjoying life to the fullest, from playing in the college band to Uncle Jake sledding with friends. The geometric pattern of layered paper in a bold palette supports this lively "slice-of-life" view of early-twentieth-century Kansas.
—Artwork: Erikia Ghumm, Brighton, Colorado

PUBLIC SALE

These simple black-and-white pages reflect the quiet dignity of a farming life in the story of a Dutch immigrant family and their move west. The family farm in Oklahoma was put up for public sale in August 1936 because the father "decided to move to another state." All Robinson family history was lost when the parents' farmhouse burned to the ground. —*Wendi Hitchings, Issaquah, Washington*

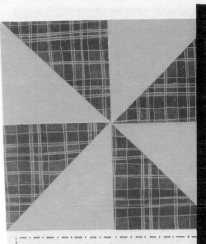

Burton Lee Pegg
- born November 24, 1873
- died February 17, 1929
- married Edna May Hatch February 25, 1914

Lee, as everyone called him, was seventeen years older than Edna. He was a friend of one of her brothers.

Lee died in a factory accident at the Henry Street plant of the Campbell Wyant and Cannon Foundry in Muskegon, Michigan. His coat got caught in a revolving mill, and when he was thrown into a pile of metal castings, he fractured a vertebrae in the lower part of his spine. He is buried in Woodland Cemetery in Reed City.

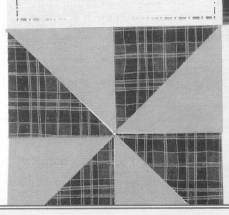

MAN'S LIFE

Burton Lee Pegg (1837–1929) was thrown to his death in a foundry accident when his coat caught in a revolving mill. The strong, simple quilt pattern frames the central images in a home-spun pattern that reflects the gentle strength of the man and the poignancy of his story.　*Debra Fee, Broomfield, Colorado*

Three Generations of
Rinaldi Family
Recipes and Memories

Kim age 5 - always
gets the first scoop!

This
Rinaldi
for a
Great Aunt
to use leftover
family orche...

Country Peach ic...

1 T. lemon juice
2 eggs
½ cup yogurt
1 cup brown sugar, packed firmly
1 t. vanilla
10-12 ripe peaches, peeled, pitted and quarte...
2 cups cream

Blend juice, eggs, yogurt, sugar and vani...
processor or blender until smooth.
Add fruit. Blend until only small pieces re...
Add cream. Pour mixture into ½ gallon ice...
freezer.
Freeze according to manufacturer's direction...
To serve top with fresh peach slices.

▲ THREE GENERATIONS OF RECIPES AND MEMORIES, KATHY STELIGO, SAN CARLOS, CALIFORNIA

Kathy has turned her passion for both food and scrapbooking into a meaningful way to preserve her family heritage—and her mother-in-law's favorite recipes!

PRESERVING FAMILY RECIPES

Scrapbookers don't have to be limited in the way they express their creativity, or their family history. Taking a look at your family's history through *your* eyes is fun and rewarding. What is *your* passion? Look at the family stories, celebrations, remembrances in that light. Do you love art, travel, theater, science, fishing, food? Find your favorite themes in your family's story and make the connections. Find a common thread. So much of our lives centers around food. Family recipes is a natural. Keepsake cookbooks combine favorite family recipes and family traditions.

Kathy Steligo of Carlos, California, a "fanatic scrapbooker and a fanatic cook," was always looking for a way to combine the two. Working side-by-side in the kitchen with her Sicilian mother-in-law, something clicked. "Every time I would cook with her, she told me wonderful stories about how she remembered cooking the same thing with her mother. It struck me that these recipes and stories were an important part of her heritage." The pages in Kathy's albums include more than just ingredients and measurements, they are also filled with photos and journaling relating to each favorite dish.

Kathy decided to compile her mother-in-law's favorite recipes into a keepsake recipe album. To record the recipes, her mother-in-law prepared each dish while Kathy measured quantities. The dishes were prepared a little differently each time because her mother-in-law never measures ingredients. With the use of a tape recorder and a home computer, Kathy documented the stories associated with each recipe using large, easy-to-read type. To get started, it's best to choose a theme, collect the recipes, record food memories, and add photos and any other illustrations.

Keepsake cookbooks make perfect gifts. Some of our fondest memories involve food. Document your family recipes along with stories, photos, and traditions. A lot of families pass things down word-of-mouth, but after one or two generations, a lot of detail gets lost. Too many people say, "I wish I had that recipe from my mother," or, "I wish I could remember that story about Grandma's fried chicken." Although the thought of assembling a large cookbook might be mind-boggling, an easy way to get started is to incorporate recipe pages in your family scrapbooks.

A very successful recipe book was one we made for a bridal shower. Each guest was asked to contribute a recipe. Each spread in the book includes a recipe and a photo of the bride with the recipe-giver, along with extra shower pictures.

Whether to type recipes or handwrite them is a matter of preference and convenience. The handwritten recipes in our recipe book add to the personal nature of the gift. Sometimes, however, it may not be practical to complete a recipe album entirely by hand. If you plan to make multiple copies of the book, you might seriously consider typing the recipes on the computer, if you don't want to have copies made of the handwritten pages.

FAMILY FAVORITES

When mother died, several of us gathered at her house to get things in order. Ann took a box of old papers and photos. That year, each of the siblings received a remarkable Christmas gift—a silver box (metal CD case, actually) wrapped with a vellum band announced *Family Favorites: Good Times, Good Thoughts, Good Food.* Each box contained a selection of favorite family recipes printed on vellum and copies of wonderful old photographs of each family member, mostly on their birthday when the tradition was to have your photograph taken while holding your homemade-by-Mom birthday cake. We had lots of family traditions—the birthday photo with cake, Dad's best-ever homegrown popcorn, hot chocolate every Sunday morning after church, Christmas popcorn balls. And Ann captured the best for us. Dad's popcorn *was* extraordinary. Every night, long after supper, we would gather around the kitchen table and share a giant pot of homegrown popcorn and family tales. Dad grew the corn, dried the kernels, and popped the corn. We had the fun of eating it. I've never tasted better popcorn. The photo on the right shows Ann pouring melted butter on a fresh batch. After Mom and Dad sold the farm and moved closer to town, Ann, then married and living farther north in Minnesota, decided to grow some corn, dry it, and give the kernels to Dad for Christmas so he could continue the family tradition of real homegrown popcorn. All went well until she went into the attic to collect the dried kernels, only to find that the mice had beaten her to it. Needless to say, we didn't have real homegrown popcorn that Christmas. I had no idea that a bunch of old photos and recipes would bring so many memories flooding back. How wonderful that I can actually *see* the church suppers and picnics with Mom's famous bars—chocolate, Rice Krispies (of course), and scotcheroos! No self-respecting proper Minnesotan would visit anyone's home or picnic without a batch or two! —*Judy Ritchie*

SCOTCHEROOS

Wayne loved these bars and Mom always made sure she had them on hand when we came to Minnesota. My recipe card looks like Wayne started to write it, but Mom finished it (she probably found a job for him to do).

> *1 cup sugar*
> *1 cup corn syrup*

Combine and bring to a boil, remove from stove, and add:

> *1 cup peanut butter*
> *5 cups Rice Krispies*

Pour into a well-buttered 9 x 12 cake pan. Put butter on your hands and pat the mixture into the pan. Melt together in a double boiler:

> *1 6-oz. package chocolate chips*
> *1 6-oz. package butterscotch chips*

Pour this mixture while still warm on top of the peanut butter and Rice Krispie mixture. Refrigerate for a few minutes to set and cool. Cut into bars and serve.

Artwork (facing page): Erikia Ghumm, Brighton, Colorado

Family Favorites

My best childhood memories are of birthdays with family. Our birthdays were always special thanks to Mom. For each birthday, she made one of her delicious cakes and made sure to get a photo of the birthday person with their cake. Today, Mom's memory lives on through her recipes that our family continues to enjoy.

SEVEN MINUTE FROSTING

2 UNBEATEN EGG WHITES
1 1/2 CUPS SUGAR
5 TBLS COLD WATER
1/4 TSP CREAM OF TARTAR
1 TSP VANILLA

BEAT ALL BUT VANILLA WITH BEATER OVER BOILING WATER FOR SEVEN MINUTES. REMOVE ICING FROM HEAT AND ADD VANILLA. CONTINUE BEATING UNTIL THE ICING IS THE RIGHT CONSISTENCY TO BE SPREAD.

5 MINUTES. REMOVE FROM HEAT AND ADD BAKING SODA. STIR WELL. POUR OVER CORN. SPREAD ON COOKIE SHEET. PLACE IN 200 DEGREE OVEN FOR 1 HOUR STIRRING AT 15 MINUTE INTERVALS. REMOVE FROM OVEN. WHEN COOL, PUT IN COVERED CONTAINER TO KEEP CRISP.

MIX SUGAR AND BEATEN EGGS. ADD MILK AND SODA MIXTURE ALTERNATELY WITH FOUR AND SALT. ADD NUTS LAST AND BAKE IN 2 LOAF PANS AT 350 DEGREES FOR ABOUT 1 HOUR.

CREAM SUGAR AND SHORTENING. ADD BEATEN EGGS AND MIX OTHER INGREDIENTS IN ORDER GIVEN. BE SURE TO CHOP THE PEANUTS. SHAPE INTO BALLS AND FLATTEN. BAKE IN MODERATE OVEN.

STIR UNTIL BATTER IS SMOOTH. PLACE 1 TOP BATTER ON PREHEATED KRUMKAKE IRON. CLOSE COVER, PRESS HANDLES TOGETHER SLIGHTLY TO PRESS BATTER. BAKE ON LOW HEAT ABOUT 3 MINUTES. TURN IRON AS IT BAKES OR UNTIL KRUMKAKE IS DELICATELY BROWN. MAKES ABOUT 2 DOZEN.

3 CUPS FLOUR

MIX INGREDIENTS IN ORDER GIVEN. ROLL OUT AND CUT WITH COOKIE CUTTERS. BAKE AT 350 DEGREES.

Family Favorites

GOOD TIMES, GOOD THOUGHTS, GOOD FOOD
MERRY CHRISTMAS 1999

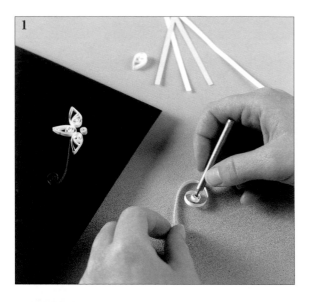

QUILLING

Creative scrapbookers find inspiration in many places. Quilling adds sculptural dimension to your pages. The effect is sophisticated and dramatic. Quilling is a simple decorative technique that you can use to embellish any kind of page—whether it's formal or casual fun. You simply roll thin strips of paper into various shapes and then arrange and combine the shapes to make your design. You can make flower centers and teardrop petals, leaves, scrolls, and stems. You can glue designs together, too, to form borders and garlands of flowers. The standard size for quilling paper is 1/8 inch, but wider and thinner sizes are available, too. You'll also need glue and a slotted or needle tool around which you can roll the paper.

1. Cut a strip of paper to the desired length—shorter for smaller shapes, longer for larger shapes. Moisten one end of the strip and place that end against your index finger. Position the needle tool on the end of the paper. Press the end of the paper around the tool with your thumb. Hold the tool steady and roll the paper, keeping the edges of the strip as even as possible.

2. To make a tight circle, roll the strip around the tool. Slip the tool from the roll's center and hold the roll to keep it from unwinding. Glue the loose end of the paper to the side of the roll. To make a loose circle, simply let the roll loosen slightly when you remove the tool.

3. To make a teardrop leaf, pinch one side of a loose circle to form a point. To make a scroll, roll only one end of the strip and leave the other end loose. To make a V scroll, crease the strip at its center and roll each end away from the crease.

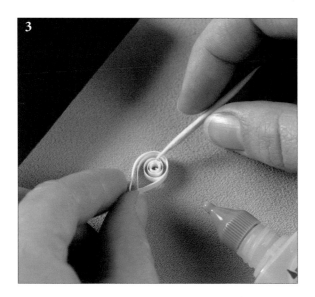

TIP

Remember, when you want to use a quilling technique to create embellishments for your page, the smaller the tool, the tighter the roll. When adding such a dimensional accent to the page, less is definitely more. Small accents are more effective than massive areas of ornamentation.

▶ WEDDING PARTY, AMANDA WILSON, COLORADO SPRINGS, COLORADO

Old wedding photos or group portraits—from every era—invoke sweet memories of bygone days. The delicate quilled embellishments add to the elegance.

Jean K. (Brightman) Camire   Sandra J. Kent   Antoinette Dehullu   Kathleen P. (Kennedy) Wilson   Douglas E. Wilson Jr.   Ronald J. Wilson   Richard D. Kennedy   Harry Briggs III   John E. Wilson Jr.

September 7, 1968
North Parish Church
North Andover, MA

In the photo album, handwritten captions read:

Lucy and Ryan with lilacs and roses 1998

Beautiful as a Rosebud Sarah 1998

▲ BEAUTIFUL AS A ROSEBUD, PHOTO: CHERYL WINSOR FOR THE MARSHALL COMPANY

Sarah's charming black-and-white portrait comes to life with soft hand-tinted colors, applied sparingly to create a dreamy, nostalgic effect.

HANDCOLORING PHOTOGRAPHS

The small finishing touches on a scrapbook page are often what make the page. A gentle touch of color wiped onto black-and-white photos are one most attractive way to refine the finished product. Black-and-white photos can be beautifully and subtly enhanced by a soft tint of color applied sparingly, and a new photo can be give an "aged" look when touched with a hint of hand coloring.

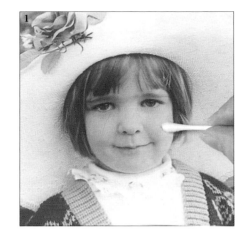

You can add soft, hand-tinted color to any of your black-and-white or sepia-tone photographs. Be sure that the photo has a matte or semi-matte finish. If you would rather not work on the original photographs—particularly old, one-of-a-kind photographs—have the photo lab make reprints or make copies on a color copying machine. Choose photo oil color paints in the colors you'll need—white, red, blue, black, yellow—and any other colors that appeal to you. You won't need much paint, so buy small tubes.

Squirt a small amount of each color you want to use on tracing paper, wax paper, or palette paper. You'll also need cotton balls, cotton swabs, and toothpicks; a utility knife; and a white, nonabrasive eraser. Put a few sheets of drawing paper underneath your photograph as a cushion.

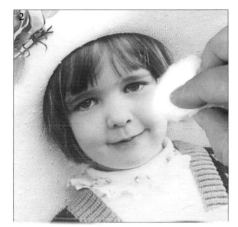

You can apply color to the whole photograph or to one small area. You can mix any of the colors before you apply them, or blend them on the photo. Subtle colors will create a nostalgic look; stronger colors will be more dramatic.

1. To apply color, put a tiny amount of paint on a cotton swab. Tap off the excess paint. Gently rub the color in the desired area in a circular motion. If you are working on small, detailed areas, wrap the tip of a toothpick with a little cotton to apply the color.

2. If the color is too bright, gently rub the area with a clean cotton ball to tone down the color. The more you rub, the lighter the tint. Don't worry about staying in the "lines." If one color washes over the edge of another, work the first color again in that area.

3. You can also erase photo oils before they dry! To remove color in a large area, simply rub it off with a clean cotton ball. To remove color along edges and in small areas (teeth and eyes, for example), use the edge of a white, nonabrasive erase. (To keep the edge of your eraser sharp as you work, trim it with a utility knife. Clean the eraser from time to time, too, by rubbing it on a clean rag.)

As soon as the oil paint dries, the color is permanent. If you have only lightly tinted the image, you can usually handle the photograph in a few days. If you have applied a lot of paint —and depending on the paper type and humidity—you may have to wait a few weeks before handling the photograph.

▲ DIE CUT WINDOW FRAME, ARTWORK: PAM KLASSEN, WESTMINSTER, COLORADO, PHOTO: MICHELE GERBRANDT

Frames are always important. But frames with a "twist" add extra dimension. Creative scrapbookers add new dimensions with materials and techniques. This scrapbooker has taken a commercially available die-cut frame and created a center-opening window frame by mounting the white frame on black paper and cutting down the center through both layers to form two window halves. Then she cut out the inside edges of each half to form a window through which we see the wedding portrait underneath. Each half of the die-cut window frame is then hinged to the outside edges of the portrait page.

Daisy Butcher Slater

Paul Raymond Slater

Legacy

Paul & Daisy Slater began a family connection to China that has spanned four generations. Little did they know what they began when they became Medical Missionaries in 1930, moving to Peiping, (Beijing today) China & later moving to Nantong, where

Passport Photo 1938: Paul, Daisy, Mary Jo, Bill & Joy

they raised 3 of their 5 children. As a doctor/nurse team in the turbulent 1930's they had experiences that would have made a great book or movie. Including finding a tiny baby on their doorstep left by a mother looking for a better life for her child. They nicknamed the baby "Tootsie" & found her a loving home. "Tootsie" again when she visited

50 years later, your grandma Mary saw Nantong. Paul & Daisy left China only when the war with Japan made it too dangerous to stay & returned to the U.S.A in early 1941. Paul & Daisy passed along to their children & grandchildren a love & respect for the beauty & history of China. When your Daddy & I wanted to adopt our family we knew we'd find our daughters in China. We adopted your sister Mary in 1997 and you in 2000. The two best things we've ever had happen to us! We gave you a Chinese middle name "DaiXi" to honor your great-grandmother Daisy. I'd like to think Paul & Daisy were watching out for us and helped guide us to you and your sister. What an incredible journey we took to be your family — a journey that began back in 1930 with Paul & Daisy!

Sisters: Mary & Claire 2000

LEGACY

Clare, adopted in China in 2000, has been given a Chinese middle name "DaiXi" to honor Great-Grandmother Daisy, who lived in China in the 1930s as a medical missionary and who loved the country with all her heart. Daisy's spirit will not be forgotten; and her love of China—its beauty and history—will continue for many more generations. —*Melanie Mitchell, Overland Park, Kansas*

September 3, 1934
Mr. and Mrs. Anthony A. Aurelia

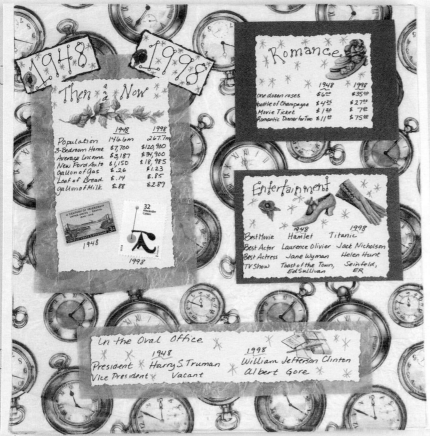

▲ 50TH ANNIVERSARY, SANDRA VAN HEUSEN, ST. CLAIR SHORES, MICHIGAN

To celebrate her in-laws' 50th anniversary, Sandra created a page that compared the popular shows, presidents, and prices in the year the couple got married to the same in the year of their golden anniversary.

▶ MARRIAGE CERTIFICATE, LINDA MILLIGAN, EL PASO, TEXAS

Historical documents add special interest to your heritage pages. Make photocopies so that you don't damage the originals— which you will want to keep in a safe place. Reduce or enlarge the documents to fit your page.

◀ ANTHONY AND MARION, KATHERINE AURELIA, KOKOMO, INDIANA

This simple and delicate wedding portrait was matted with green paper and lace-paper stickers and trimmed with a corner rounder punch.

▲ WELCOME HOME JIM,
NANCY CHEARNO-STERSHIC,
BEL AIR, MARYLAND

This patriotic page celebrates the day "Jimmy came home from the war." The vintage photos are matted with red, white, and blue. The stars are punched, and the banner is cut freehand.

◄ AT SEA AND ON SHORE,
LINDA MILLIGAN, EL PASO, TEXAS

Literally rows of simply matted candid snapshots flood the page capturing sailors' lives on land and sea. Journaled captions bring the images all together.

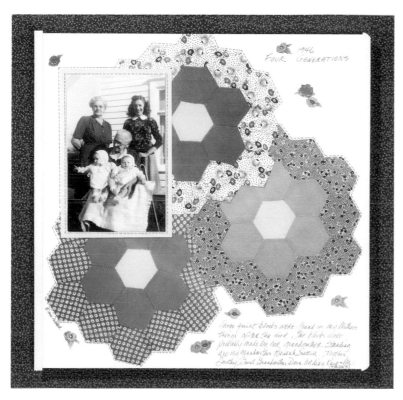

▲ FOUR GENERATIONS, FAYE WEBER, BOISE, IDAHO

When their mother died, Faye and her sister found a box of quilt blocks among her things. The fabrics were from the 1930s and 1940s, and Faye thought the blocks might have been made by her great-grandmother. Faye washed and pressed the blocks and then photocopied them. She arranged the copies into a pieced quilt pattern and added photographs of her twin sister and herself, her mother, grandmother, and great-grandmother. Faye kept the real fabric blocks to later make into a quilt project.

▲ MADE ESPECIALLY FOR ME, JUDY WESTON, POPLAR BLUFF, WISCONSIN

When Judy was a little girl, her grandmother, who lived to be 103 years old, made her a Sunbonnet Sue quilt. Just a few years ago on a trip to New York City, Judy found a Sunbonnet Sue rubber stamp, which she used with colorful inks to decorate this page honoring her grandmother. A photograph of the actual quilt is at the center, surrounded by variously cropped, matted, and framed photographs of Grandmother Moll at various stages of her life.

FIVE GENERATIONS OF YOUNG WOMEN
(following spread)

In a box of photos old and new, we found a portrait of a woman I had never seen before. I had heard stories of the strength of the McCormick women. This photo turned out to be of my mother's mother's mother. There certainly is strength in her face. And then, the appealing image of my mother and her twin sister with their mother in a rather formal studio portrait reiterated the relaxed, casual air my mother possessed, while her sister was ever demure. I couldn't resist adding on photos of my daughter and me. There *is* a line to be traced. Maybe someone in a future generation will continue the line. I'd love to see the progression. —*Ellen Maher, artwork: Erikia Ghumm, Brighton, Colorado*

Five Generations of Young Women

Margaret 1900

Every baby born into this world is a finer one than the last.
—CHARLES DICKENS

Leslie 1943

Eileen 1911

Elen 1911

Eunice 1911

Maria 1972

Each bell was attached to a present

Seth in his tree hat

Seth & his friend Walter do a craft

Seth's class has a Happy Birthday Jesus party

TODAY: MAKING MEMORIES

W e make memories every day. Some of our most memorable days are special and festive occasions—weddings, birthdays, holiday celebrations. These bright days are full of wonderful foods, lively games, music, and color—and warm and lasting memories for everyone who is there to enjoy them. Most scrapbooks are full of pages that record these happy times in words and pictures.

Most of our days, however, are just ordinary ones—filled with familiar routines. In some ways, these are the days that we remember most fondly. We often take them for granted, but our day-to-day lives are filled with significant moments. In time, these simple memories will be especially meaningful. Our everyday activities reveal the close bonds that we share with other family members—gathered around the dinner table, cooking together in the kitchen, reading a book, caring for someone who is under the weather, building sand castles on the beach.

Perhaps this was the last Thanksgiving you celebrated with an elderly grandparent; or maybe a family member was ill or too far away to join the festivities. Maybe a favorite grandparent told a poignant story showing his or her strength and resolve—a story demonstrating grace in the face of hardship. These, too, are moments you will want to capture and remember. You'll start to see your everyday world in a new light. And if you catch a bit of nostalgia, so much the better.

◄ CHRISTMAS SAMPLER, MARILYN GARNER, SAN DIEGO, CALIFORNIA

The bright colors and playful shapes and accents of this sampler quilt page add a touch of whimsy to holiday school memories. The "stitch" lines are drawn with ink. Crisp, clean Christmas shapes, cut with seasonal templates and filled with appropriately cropped photos, surround a central colorful pieced-paper Santa figure.

▲ THE MEMORIES THAT TOUCH OUR HEARTS, DAWN MABE, BROOMFIELD, COLORADO

Rather than assembling this patchwork-quilt page with glue, Dawn actually stitched the squares together on her sewing machine. Stitching paper will eventually dull your needle, but you can make a few pages before you have to replace it, and it definitely adds authenticity.

THE CHANGING SEASONS

Many scrapbook artists choose the cycle of changing seasons as the organizing theme for their pages. Each of the four seasons has its own color schemes, motifs, holidays, traditions, and activities. The sights and sensations associated with each one of them can provide you with fresh sources of design inspiration. A summer's day at the beach suggests seashells and blue skies. The early days of autumn signal that it's nearly time to carve a pumpkin—or bake a pumpkin pie. A sudden snowstorm fills the mind's eye with fluffy white mounds and crackling ice crystals. The sudden arrival of daffodils announces the coming of spring. Let these seasonal objects, colors, and ideas be the centerpieces of your layouts, and your scrapbook will soon be filled with lively pages. There's still another advantage to seasonal scrapbooking. At least four times a year, as one season ends and another begins, you'll have extra incentive to get busy making pages.

▶ MAKING A SCARECROW, *(top)* DONNA COMMONS, JACKSONVILLE, FLORIDA

If at first you don't succeed—this artist was so caught up in the moment, she forgot to take the picture! Her accommodating young sons took their scarecrow apart and rebuilt him so she could record the moment in her scrapbook page.

▶ HOLLY, *(bottom)* KELLEY BLONDIN, GRAND BLANC, MICHIGAN

While shopping for supplies, this scrapbook artist spotted a perfect photo opportunity. The outside of the craft store was decorated for fall—so, she seized the moment and set her daughter Holly down for a portrait. The autumnal colors of the quilt block, letter, and pumpkin stickers accent the seasonal theme.

◀ PILES OF SMILES, TRISH TILDEN, WESTMONT, ILLINOIS, AND TINA WEATHERHEAD, WOODRIDGE, ILLINOIS

Tumbling leaves, made from photographs punched with a leaf-shaped punch, surround smiling faces silhouetted against out brown paper to re-create the playful sense of a joyful jump into the leaves.

▲ AT THE BEACH, Susan Walker, Oakbrook Terrace, Illinois

Hand-coloring adds soft tints to black-and-white photographs. Stenciled starfish and seashell shapes are cut out of pastel papers.

▶ HILTON BEACH, Jenny Lowhar, Miami, Florida

A summertime image of a child contentedly digging in the sand at the seashore is warm enough to keep the winter chills and blahs at more than arm's length.

▶▶ WATER FUN, Charlotte Wilhite, Fort Worth, Texas

Learning to swim is a milestone in your child's life—and in yours. With the help of an underwater disposable camera, colored papers, colored pens, a circle template, and fish stickers, this scrapbook artist recorded her four-year-old son's adventures under water. The journaling lines are song lyrics from the Disney film The Little Mermaid.

Under the sea, just you and me. Baby, it's better, down where it's wetter. Take it from me...
—Sebastian, in The Little Mermaid

Water Fun!

August '94

▲ THANKSGIVING, KATHY GUIER, DOWNEY, CALIFORNIA

This scrapbooker created the mottled look of autumn leaves by sponging fall colors onto neutral-colored paper. The leaves were punched and then textured with a paper crimper. Her family's Thanksgiving memories, matted in circle shapes, float like falling leaves around the tree.

▶ PUMPKIN PATCH, LISSA MITCHELL, KANSAS CITY, MISSOURI

This cheerful, seasonal pumpkin was created with a puzzle template—an easy way to frame your photos.

ILLUSION PAGES

1. Enlarge the pattern below to a size that fits your scrapbook page (this hexagonal pattern is from the book *Triad Optical Illusions* by Harry Turner, Dover Publications, 1978). Make a copy of the pattern so you can refer to it as you work.

2. Each of the six blocks is made of three shaded sections. Choose light, medium, and dark papers to work with to show the shading. Cut out the three sections of one of the blocks. Trace each shaded piece onto colored or printed paper that matches the degree of shading. Reassemble the block and tape the pieces in place.

3. Now, choose your photos. Match the shade of each photo with the shade of its mat to add to the three-dimensional effect. Working on a lightbox, trace the pattern over the photograph. Trim the photograph about ¼ inch on all sides and mount it on the mat. Crop and mat each photo—including the center photo.

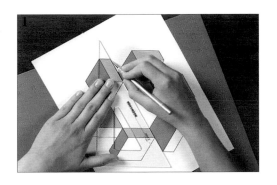

▲ PUMPKIN HARVEST, ARTWORK: CONNIE MIEDEN (COX), WESTMINSTER, COLORADO, PHOTOS: SANDRA ESCOBEDA, MANTECA, CALIFORNIA

Create the illusion of depth and light with a few tricks of perspective and some simple supplies.

▲ **SNOW BOARDERS**, Kathleen Paneitz, Longmont, Colorado

···

This delightful winter scene uses accents of vellum perfectly. The icy letters cut from dark blue paper and realistic snowflakes in a dark blue sky are finished with a layer of cut vellum.

◄ **SNOWMAN**, TerryAnn Benedict, Belt, Montana

···

A simple, wreath-shaped design made with a circle template makes a playful page of memories for the proud builder of this snowman. The snowman's nose, eyes, and mouth are cut out with deckle-edged scissors, and his cutout top hat completes his classic look.

► **SNOWY DAYS**, Dorothy Ferreira, Woodcliff Lake, New Jersey

···

This scrapbook artist is also a quilter, so she made a "warm and cozy quilt" of her pictures of her children's snowy days, juxtaposing photos and illustrations.

SNOWY

DAYS

Winter 1994 brought more
snow for us to play with.
Shelby was big enough
to really enjoy
it all. Jay
would use his
plow to make big
piles of snow for the
kids to make igloos with.

SNOW ♥

Zoryana At the
Lake Tahoe Cabin
on her 6th
Birthday 2000

► WINTER STREAM, Pamela Zenger, Spokane, Washington

A line of verse from the Book of Psalms adds to the reflective mood of this quiet winter scene. Die cuts, deckle scissored paper, and small punched snowflakes and leaves accent the black-and-white photo to create the wintry effect.

◄ SNOW, Oksanna Pope, Los Gatos, California

Remember that snowy sixth birthday? This sparkling page brightens the photos—and the memory of a wintry day at Lake Tahoe—with a background that echoes the colors and textures of the photographs.

▼ BLAME IT ON EL NIÑO, Jeanne Ciolli, Dove Canyon, California

The unexpected thrill of a sudden snowstorm in April made these skiers' day! To make the most of her theme, Jeanne iced her pages with mounds of decorative die-cut snowflakes.

As the deer pants for water, so my soul thirsts for thee, O God
Psalms 42:1

Blame it on El Niño!

this is April? Wow!

Welcome to MOUNT PLUTO ELEVATION 8,610

Thanks to the El Niño storms of 1998, we watched as over two feet of fresh snow was added to the existing 7-14 foot base on the Northstar slopes.

PUNCHED FLOWERS

LARGE FLOWERS: Old tree, medium apple, small heart, 1/8-inch round hand punch. Punch and assemble as shown. For the softened edge effect, gently roll the edges of the flowers and leaves around a pencil before placing on the page. A medium butterfly punch finished the page.

LILACS: Small heart, diamond mini extension, negative squares from southwest border, 1/16-inch round hand punch. Punch and assemble as shown.

LARGE FLOWER BUDS: Old tree, medium heart. Punch and assemble as shown.

▲ BUTTERFLIES & BLOOMS, ARTWORK: PAM KLASSEN, WESTMINSTER, COLORADO, PHOTO: ERICIA PIEROVICH, LONGMONT, COLORADO

A portrait photograph and layers of punched lilacs, flowers, and butterflies turn Alexandra's summer of 1998 into a lush, blossom-filled garden.

▶ SPRING PORTRAITS, MARILYN GARNER, SAN DIEGO, CALIFORNIA

Simple presentations sometimes call out for an unusual, decorative touch. These fanciful flowers add a touch of spring when used as borders or frames to such inviting outdoor portraits. Use the folded floral shapes alone or in clusters.

FOLDED FLOWERS

Cut a circle of colored paper with a circle cutter or template (this sample is 2 1/8 inches in diameter). Fold the circle in half, then fold it in half again to form a quarter circle.

Unfold the quarter circle so that the paper is a half circle again. Now fold the outer edge of each quarter circle into the center crease. Fold the edges in again. Now unfold the paper so that it is a full circle. On the back side of the circle, mark and number each crease from 1 to 16, working clockwise, as shown

To complete the folded flower, follow this sequence of steps: Fold crease 10 to 12. Fold 7 to 9. Fold 4 to 6. Crease the flower at 2 and 13. Layer each folded flower beneath a punched green bell, as shown.

Miss Hannah 1999

THE DRESDAN PLATE

To make your template, draw a circle to fit your page. Then draw another circle within it to the size you want your central photograph to be. Divide the outer circle into sixteen or twenty equal parts. These will form the "fans" of the plate.

1. Using the pattern below, make a template for the segments. Trace the shape onto printed paper.

2. Cut the shapes. For this design, you'll need sixteen pieces.

3. Find and lightly mark the center of your page with a pencil. Draw a 1-inch-diameter circle at the center of the page. Arrange the fans around the small circle, making sure they are aligned.

Crop your photo to the desired size. Add a mat and adhere the photo to the center of the page. Add a title below the photo if you wish.

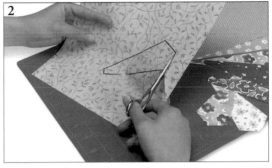

◄ ◄ MISS HANNAH, Marilyn Garner, San Diego, California

This cheerful page features a portrait of Hannah in her sunbonnet, framed by colorful prints arranged in the pattern of a traditional Dresdan Plate quilt pattern, which was popular in the 1930s and 1940s.

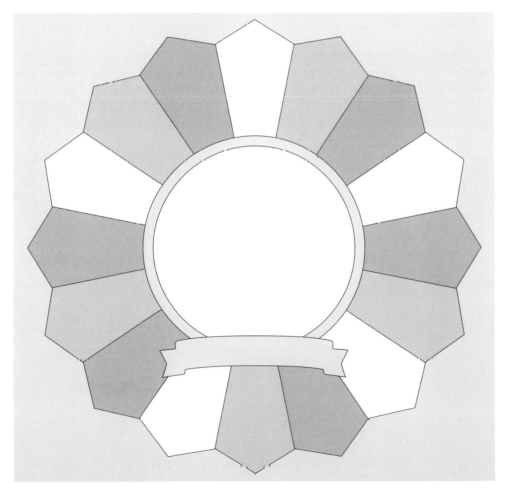

OUR

FAMILY

TRADITIONS

1999

A TREASURED PHOTO
OF
STRAWBERRY & TYSON

JANUARY

HAVING A VALENTINES
LUNCH WITH MY FRIENDS
FROM COLLEGE.

THE FAMILY
HELD AT OU
THE FOURT

FEBRUARY

MARCH

OCTOBER

A BIRTHDAY PHOTO
COMPLETE WITH CAKE
AND BALLOONS.

APRIL

OUR
ALW

ANNUAL EASTER EGG HUNT
WITH OUR COUSINS.

JUNE

EVERYBODY GETS BREAKFAST
IN BED ON THEIR BIRTHDAY.

AT TH
TURKE

SUMMER
CALIFORNIA
& GRANDMA'S BEACH HOU

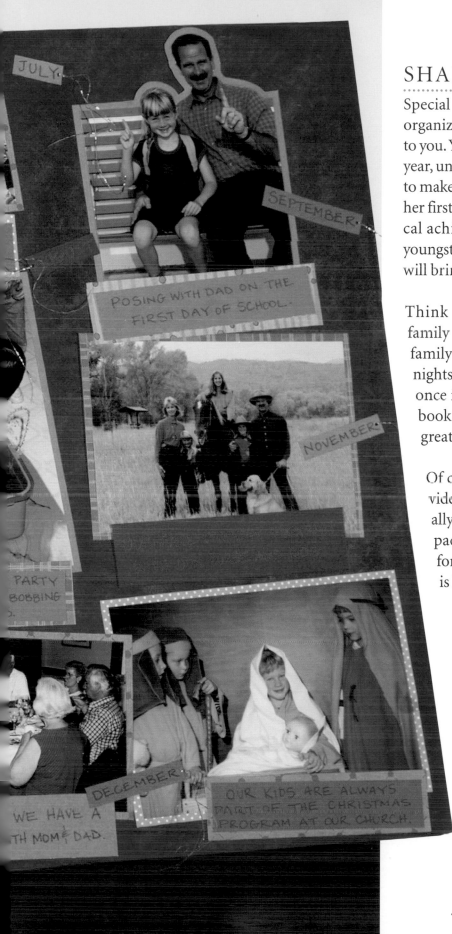

SHARED MOMENTS, SPECIAL EVENTS

Special family events provide another rich theme around which to organize the pages of your scrapbook. How you define special is up to you. You might want to record your son's first days of school—every year, until the year he graduates from high school. Or you might want to make much of the day that your little girl lost her first tooth or read her first chapter book all by herself. Special sports, academic, or musical achievements—like the home team's winning games or your youngster's violin recital—also make wonderful themes for pages that will bring pride and joy for years to come.

Think about those simple, special events that you and your family share as a group, too. Is there something that you and your family especially like to do together? Pizza and a movie on Friday nights? Canoe trips on the lake every other Sunday? Visits to the zoo once in a while? Whatever the activity is, record it in your scrapbook. Because they are shared, even the simplest moments have a great significance in your family's life.

Of course, family vacations are shared events, too, and they provide myriad themes for your scrapbook pages. Your camera is usually at the ready—and there are plenty of colorful sights, action-packed adventures, and special moments to record. And don't forget to document the road trip, too—sometimes getting there is half the fun!

◂ OUR FAMILY TRADITIONS, ARTWORK: ERIKIA GHUMM, BRIGHTON, COLORADO, PHOTOS: JOYCE FEIL, GOLDEN, COLORADO

Special events happen all year round. See for yourself. Try scrapbook pages that celebrate—in words and pictures—the traditions your family shares each month of the year.

► PIZZA NIGHT, ARTWORK: PAM KLASSEN, WESTMINSTER, COLORADO, PHOTOS: PENNIE STUTZMAN, BROOMFIELD, COLORADO

Even the simplest traditions are worth preserving—like Saturday morning breakfasts or Friday pizza nights.

►► BABTSIA'S PASKA, OKSANNA POPE, LOS GATOS, CALIFORNIA

Oksanna scrapbooked about a favorite Ukranian Easter tradition that centers around paska, a special type of bread her mother bakes every year for the event.

▼ SCHOOLBUS CAKE, DEBBIE LAITINEN, SEYMOUR, INDIANA

When Tyler came home from his first day of school, Debbie surprised him with a cake she had baked just for him—in the shape of a schoolbus! She has since celebrated every one of her kids' first day of school the same way.

HOW TO PRESERVE TRADITIONS

Traditions do not have to be complex rituals passed down from your ancestors. Many families create traditions of their own: movie nights, special birthday breakfasts, annual photos on the front porch. No matter the size or significance of your traditions, include them in your scrapbook. Here are some hints for preserving them:

Photograph elements of your tradition at least once—special food, activities, preparations?

• JOURNAL. The only way to pass on the reason behind the tradition is through words. Write down the origin of the tradition. When did it begin and why? Don't feel obligated to pen lengthy paragraphs; bulleted information works just as well.

• INCLUDE PEOPLE. What role does each family member play in the tradition? Even if it's just as the movie-picker-outer for family movie night or the babysitter for your weekly date night, include each person's photo and journal about his or her role.

• INCORPORATE COLORS. If specific colors are significant in the tradition, use them in the page design. There are traditional colors—red and green for Christmas, blue or silver at Hanukkah—or your family might have special colors to wear each year for family photos. Make a frame or background using the colors and journal about their significance.

• HIGHLIGHT SYMBOLS. Photograph or enlarge symbols closely associated with your traditions. Remember to include a description of their meaning if you know it.

• TALK TO OLDER RELATIVES. If the tradition is an old one, and the significance is unknown, interview older family members to find out if they know the origin. Include memories of traditions by younger members as well.

SATURDAY MORNINGS, MICHELE GERBRANDT, WESTMINSTER, COLORADO

Traditions don't always revolve around the holidays. Our daily routines and special weekly events also make wonderful memories. Every Saturday morning, I make fresh popovers for my family—just like my mom always did. I never thought of this routine as a "family tradition," until my husband called it one. So, I created a pop-up popover page for my scrapbook—featuring my daughter Anna, who is carrying on the tradition by learning to make popovers, too!

EVERY SATURDAY MORNING POPOVERS

① SET OVEN TO 400°

④ MIX TOGETHER

② GREASE MUFFIN PAN

③ GATHER INGREDIENTS

POP-UP PAGES

For a lively layout, make your pages jump up and out, pop-up, or peek-a-boo. Choose a pop-up feature that matches your theme.

1. Copy the pop-up template on page 140, or draw your own to fit your album. Fold the template along the center fold line. Fold the tabs up along the fold line.

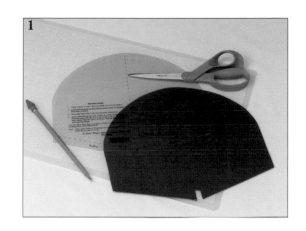

2. Crop your photograph to the shape of the pop-up. For these pages, the popover was drawn freehand, cut as a separate piece, and attached to the back of the photograph. Fold the photograph and the popover along the pop-up fold lines. Fold the bottom edges along the tab folds.

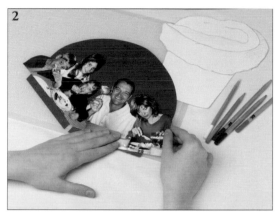

3. Fold the pop-up along the center fold line. Fold tabs up along the bottom edge. Measure the gap between the pages in the album you are using. Position the left and right pages so that the center gap is the same width. It's important that each side of the pop-up stand is positioned in the exact location on opposite pages.

To accomplish this, make sure the notched end of the base is approximately 3 inches down from the upper edge of the page. Then angle out so the opposite ends of the base fall approximately 2 to 3 inches away from the gutter at the upper edge of the page. Pencil mark this location, then adhere the pop-up to your page. When you close the album, the stand should fold neatly to the interior of the two-page spread.

TIP

For extra dimension and detail, decorate your pop up with die cuts, punched shapes, colored drawings, and journaling.

◄ FOUR GENERATIONS OF GERBRANDTS, ARTWORK: KATHLEEN PANEITZ, PHOTO: JOYCE FEIL, GOLDEN, COLORADO

At last they meet! Grandpa Gerbrandt traveled from California to Colorado to meet his new great-grandson, Daniel. Of his fourteen great-grandchildren, only two of the boys share his name. This portrait shows the four generations of fathers and sons who carry on the Gerbrandt family name: Daniel, his father Ron, his grandfather Gordon, and, of course, his great-grandfather Abe.

▼ FRIENDS & FAMILY, CLAUDIA HILL, WHITTIER, CALIFORNIA

Solid and patterned printed paper mats, stickers aplenty, die-cut frames, intriguingly cut photos, frames, and mats all contribute to a vibrant and fun-filled picture of contemporary family life from holidays and vacations to everyday moments.

▲ FOUR GENERATIONS, TWYLA STAIR, LUBBOCK,
TEXAS

Lauren and Meredith love to spend time with Great Granny on her farm.
Patterned papers in gingham and plaid add a homey touch to these generation pages made for the girls by their mother, Twyla. The ribbons are cut
freehand. The bows are made with a template. Both are boldly outlined
and detailed with a thick black pen. The journaling is done with a more
delicate line.

▶ GRANDMA'S GIFT TO AMY, ARTWORK: PAM
KLASSEN, WESTMINSTER, COLORADO

A simple presentation is as effective as a more elaborate one when the
moment speaks for itself. A devoted grandma who knows just what is on
the mind of her second youngest grandchild has a special gift for the little
girl on the occasion of her baby sister's christening. The candid photograph is simply cropped and presented on a background of punched pastel printed papers beneath a layer of soft vellum—a lovely way to remember a tender moment on a special family day.

SISTERS IN SPIRIT

MacKenzie 3 yrs. old

ADOPTION DAY.

ELEVEN LITTLE GIRLS WERE ADOPTED FROM CHINA ON THE SAME DAY. ALTHOUGH THEY LIVE FAR APART, THEIR PARENTS HELP THEM REMAIN CONNECTED BY GETTING TOGETHER ONCE A YEAR.

A REUNION 3 YEARS LATER. GIRLS SETTING IN SAME ORDER.

JULIA
3 YRS. OLD

SISTERS IN SPIRIT

Every year, eleven little Chinese girls—who were all adopted on the same day—travel from all over the United States to gather together again. These "sisters in spirit" spend the day playing, while forging a special bond that will last a lifetime. The photographs at left show the infants in a row on adoption day in Guangzhou, China, and then, three years later, as toddlers, seated in the same order in the U.S. —*Artwork: Erikia Ghumm, Brighton, Colorado, photos: Jamie Kilmartin*

A MAP OF A JOURNEY of love and faith ~ led by God, traveled by Lindsay and Peter to find Xiaoling and bring her home, to her place in the family, now complete.

A BOOK ABOUT ME, ARTWORK: PAM KLASSEN, WESTMINSTER, COLORADO, PHOTO: LORALEE DISCHNER, DENVER, COLORADO

For writers, there's an old saying, "Write about what you know best." For scrapbookers, it's not much different. Sometimes the best place to start your family story is with yourself!

GRADUATED PAGES

To create these pages, you'll need a spiral-bound album. Place wavy stickers along the edges of the second page in the album. Allow the stickers to overlap at the corners. With a straight-edged ruler and a craft knife, miter the corners of the intersecting stickers to form a clean angle. Cut away the excess strips of the stickers.

Now, with scissors, trim the page close to the edges of the border stickers. Next, measure the distance from the page's edge to the inside of the sticker. Trim the first page of the album to that measurement—so that its edge will align with the inside edge of the border sticker on the second page.

If you want to add a colored vellum insert, cut the vellum to the size of the album. Lay the paper next to the spiral binding. With pencil, mark the location of the spirals on the vellum. Now punch over the marks with a square punch. Make slits from the edge of the paper into the punched spaces. Insert the vellum sheet behind the second, wavy-bordered page.

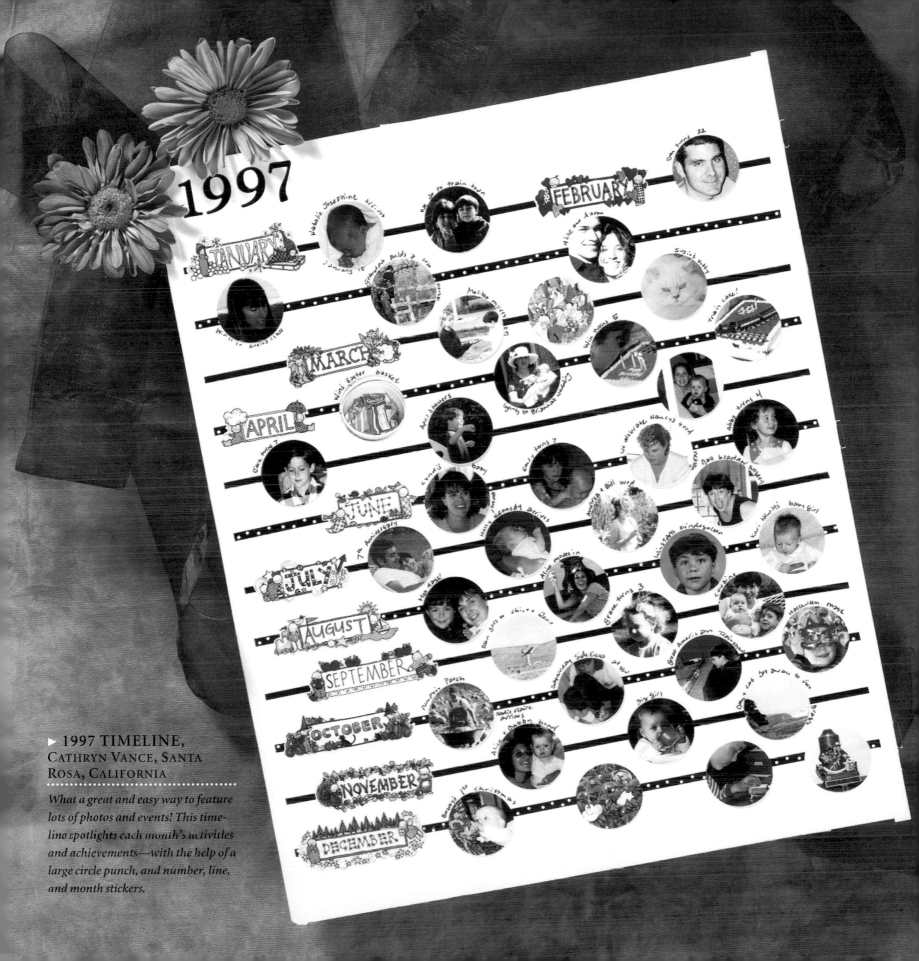

▶ 1997 TIMELINE,
CATHRYN VANCE, SANTA
ROSA, CALIFORNIA

What a great and easy way to feature lots of photos and events! This time-line spotlights each month's activities and achievements—with the help of a large circle punch, and number, line, and month stickers.

▶ HAPPY HEARTS, Teresa Villanueva, Aurora, Colorado

With colored-paper appliqués and drawn "stitch" lines, this simple quilt page presents four cheerful portraits.

◀ HUGS & KISSES, Charla Campbell, Springfield, Missouri

This Valentine's Day page features two portraits, simply sweetened by the accents of bright red against the neutral black-and-white color scheme. The roses in the photos were cut from color prints of the same scenes and positioned in exactly the same places on the black-and-white prints. The photos sit on a lacy mat cut with decorative-edged scissors and detailed with drawn black lines. The matted photos sit on a deep red, textured paper with soft, feathery edges. Cut-out hearts on white mats trimmed with scallop scissors hold the hand-lettering for the title. Punched and layered circles form the roses that are scattered on the "ground."

▲ ST. MARGARET'S SCHOOL, ARTWORK: ERIKIA GHUMM, BRIGHTON, COLORADO, PHOTOS: TRACY KOZLOWSKI, SAN CLEMENTE, CALIFORNIA

Tracy made an appreciation album for her son's preschool teacher. The brightly colored schoolhouse has fold-open doors and windows that reveal photographs of the whole gang.

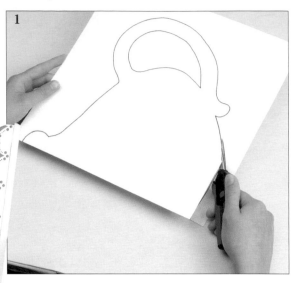

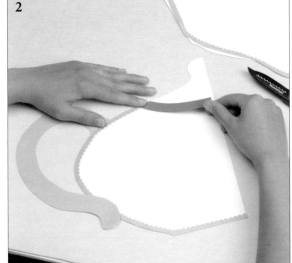

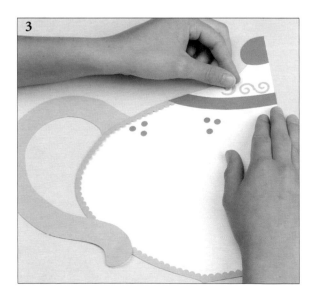

TEAPOT CUT-OUT PAGES

Here's a clever way to get lots of photos and birthday cards into just a few pages. Make the teapot pages first, then place them into the scrapbook pages.

1. Working with the template on page 140, cut out the teapot halves from white scrapbook pages. Center the page hinges.

2. With scallop scissors, cut pink strips as a border for the edges of the teapot. Cut pink handles and curved blue strips and circles for the lid.

3. Punch and arrange small pink swirls to decorate the lid. Punch ¹/4-inch blue circles to decorate the pot. When you have attached the teapot to the pages, crop and mat the photos. Journal with pink pens and add punched flowers and stickers as accents. To make the page borders, cut blue and white strips with a scalloped ruler. Punch ¹/8-inch holes in the white strips. Lay the blue strips along each page edge. Lay the white strips over the blue strips. Draw black dots and dashes to connect the holes.

Chinese Tea Ceremony

One of the most important part of a wedding for Chinese people is the tea ceremony. This is the time when the marriage of the couple is truly acknowledged by Chinese families. Because this was a tradition for my family, the tea ceremony was performed at my parents' house. Our entire family got together and dim sum & other goodies were set out for the feast. After I put on my red silk gown & red satin shoes, I hid and waited for my groom to come and get me. My grandma stayed with me to protect me while we are all waiting for him to come. Since I am the eldest daughter, this was a very special time for our family.

9.27.98

KNOCK KNOCK

KNOCK KNOCK

KNOCK KNOCK!

Randall had to wait quite some time before Judy would even answer the door. Then, he had to bribe Judy, Bonnie, Elbert, & Gail with red envelopes so they would let him in.

Coming In!

▲ CHINESE TEA CEREMONY,
WENDY FONG, ALEMEDA,
CALIFORNIA

Wendy's scrapbook records and celebrates the many special events that took place as part of her wedding celebration. Each page also celebrates her family heritage and traditions. On these pages, Wendy's journaling describes the importance of the tea ceremony in a Chinese wedding. The ancient traditions come to life in the present day with photographs and fond anecdotes about family and friends who shared the special ceremony, which took place in her parents' home.

◀ BIRTHDAY TEA PARTY,
SHAWN GLAHN, TEMECULA,
CALIFORNIA

In years to come, these girls will certainly cherish these lovely pages of their backyard tea party. The pastel colors, the teapot cutout, and the flowery page details perfectly portray the festive events of the day.

CHINESE TEA CEREMONY

The first thing Wendy Fong thought about when she became engaged was preserving every detail of her wedding, from traditional Chinese ceremonies to reception seating charts. She created two scrapbooks for the project describing the traditions in her journaling so their significance will never be lost. She could remember many images—including a roasted pig, lots of sweet cakes, and cups of steaming tea, but they were all jumbled and she wasn't sure of their meaning. Grandmother's advice was sought to help Wendy do everything in the traditional Chinese way. One of the most important parts of a wedding for Chinese people is the tea ceremony, during which the couple is truly acknowledged by the Chinese families. The bride, dressed in a traditional Chinese red dress, hides in her family home to wait for the groom to come and get her. Not only does the groom have to find his bride, he has to bribe family members with bright red envelopes to let him into the house. The ceremony is light-hearted and fun, and is finished off with a feast of dim sum and "other goodies."—*Wendy Fong, Alameda, California*

◄ AT THE ZOO,
MAGGIE LUNDQUIST,
WILLIS, MICHIGAN

Family outings provide the perfect subjects for scrapbook pages. To make the shapes that set off this jungle theme, Maggie worked with nature stamps that she had purchased to decorate her bathroom walls.

LAYERED STAMPING

To create the patterned background, apply ink to a swirl-shaped stamp. Tap the excess ink onto scrap paper. Randomly stamp swirls onto the background sheet.

Stamp other designs in colors of your choice. This scrapbooker stamped leaves in light blue and gray-green, flowers in magenta and salmon, swirls in blue and medium gray. Make as many designs as you'll need to frame the photos on your page.

Now cut out each shape, leaving a narrow solid border around the design.

To add more texture, punch ¹/₁₆-inch holes with a hand punch in the stamped cutouts before you mount them on the page.

▲ GREAT RENO BALLOON RACE, Elisa Purnell, Camarillo, California

These pages record the color and excitement of the hot-air balloon race itself. The photographs were cut with a diamond-shaped template and pieced together mosaic-style. The pattern makes a great design, and more photos can fit on the pages, too.

THE HOLIDAYS

As families gather around the Thanksgiving table or Christmas tree, light the Menorah, or carve the pumpkin, they are sharing the same traditions that most of us share. The holiday memories that each family creates, however, are uniquely its own. Each family has its own rituals and special observances—certain table linens that are always used, cakes that are always baked, songs that are always sung. There's no better time than the holidays to catch a glimpse of just what gives your family its special identity.

So, take out your camera—and your scrapbooking supplies. Relatives who live at a distance and don't visit often are likely to travel far to attend these festive, yearly gatherings. Your lens will find the family resemblances, capture the candid moments that deepen relationships, and record the traditional foods and activities that your family looks forward to so eagerly each year—perhaps the same kinds of food and activities your ancestors enjoyed in another land years ago.

If there are children in the family, you and your camera will no doubt seek them out. Children are the heart of the holidays. Portraits of youngsters on Santa's knee or wide-eyed around packages on Christmas Eve capture the very essence of the holiday. You can tell the story with a simple portrait matted with red and green or with an elaborately decorated page with a festooned pop-up Christmas tree. The choice is yours, and the possibilities are endless. You might decide to give thanks for your bounty of family and friends in a cornucopia filled with photographs of the Thanksgiving Day feast. Or you may decide to make a practical holiday page that literally holds a "pocketful" of Happy Hanukkah memories. And don't overlook those little holidays—the Fourth of July, Halloween, and, of course, Valentine's Day. Have fun arranging stars and stripes, pumpkins and spiders, and hearts and arrows as you design festive pages with style and memories that are all your own.

▲ BIRTHDAY CAKES, *(top)* CATHIE ALLAN, EDMONTON, ALBERTA, CANADA

Papa's birthday page features the guest of honor—the little girl whose scrapbook page this will someday be. A selective palette of shades of blue and turquoise plus a mustard yellow decorates the cheerful page with double mats, swirling die-cuts, and ornamental type. Balloons contain the basic journaling.

◄ RADIANT STAR QUILT, *(bottom)* RITA BREI, MISSION VIEJO, CALIFORNIA

This page design is based on the Feathered Star, a quilt block from the nineteenth century. The scrapbooker framed her modern photos with this traditional pattern to make a page that spans generations. In a scrapbook made for her children, this page records their grandmother's summer birthday party.

FAMILY PORTRAITS, MARGI BONTRAGER, KOKOMO, INDIANA

....

Even a few moments spent outdoors can be the inspiration for beautiful family pages. The natural setting of Florida is perfect for these flattering portraits. The cascading tree branches in the photographs inspired the scrapbooker to create a similar design on the pages themselves with punched and cut leaves.

TRICK OR TREAT, ILSA SCHRENK, TALLAHASSEE, FLORIDA

....

Bold graphic design sets off this fun-loving Halloween night celebration page. Orange mats leap off the black background. The black title squares, matted with orange, each holdand individual letter each one of which is created with a white pen or seasonal stickers. Photos and mats are cropped with pinking scissors and corner rounder. The fence, cat, and witch are all stickers.

▲ SPIDER WEB, Donna Pittard, Kingwood, Texas

Have fun with the holidays! Let your imagination run a little wild—and your pages will become extra special. On the page shown above, journaling and a special spider-web effect make the most of the memory of a two-year-old's first Halloween. The web was cut in one piece from white paper with a craft knife and mat. The photos were cropped to fit the spaces in the web. The background is black paper with a border of woodgrain paper strips.

◄ OUR BOUNTIFUL HARVEST, Donna Pittard, Kingwood, Texas

Every occasion has special symbols or traditional motifs. Make the most of them! The bounty and blessings of family are captured in this scrapbook artist's Thanksgiving Day horn of plenty. The photographs of three generations of family are cropped and matted on the fruit and vegetable shapes that spill out of the cornucopia. The photos were cropped to be slightly smaller than the autumn-colored mats. The grapes were punched from small and medium circle punches. The horn and ribbon were shaded with colored pencils and chalk. Fine details and the title lettering were drawn with colored pen.

HAPPY HANUKKAH, ILESE SCHRENK, TALLAHASSEE, FLORIDA

A pocket folder in this page holds holiday cards to preserve the greetings of family and friends. The background is a printed paper. The pocket is cut from a gold sheet and cut with deckle-edged scissors. The postage stamp and the photographs are also cut with deckle edges. Colorful Menorah stickers and journaling in white pen finish the page.

HAPPY HANUKKAH, LORIE SAVINAR, DENVER, COLORADO

The gift-giving traditions of Hanukkah inspired the simple design of this scrapbooker's holiday pages. Wallet-sized photographs of her toddler, Lorie, fit perfectly in gift boxes "tied" with bows of blue and silver metallic papers. The gift box and bow shapes are made with die cuts. The white lettering of the title was drawn with a letter template and silver pen.

hanukkah

19 99

◄ SWADDLED BABES, Charla
Campbell, Springfield, Missouri

*Inspired by baby photographer Anne Geddes, this
scrapbooker modeled her daughter Kayla in swad-
dling clothes and gingerbread and snowman costumes. The design of each page echoes the mood,
theme, colors, and textures of the photograph.*

PAPER PIECING

1. Place the poinsettia stencil on the scrapbook page so that the design is right side up. Now, turn the stencil over on a flat surface. Place colored paper on top of the stencil. Outline each shape with an embossing stylus. For light papers, work on a light table. For dark papers, emboss by feel, lifting the paper to check your work as needed.

2. Cut out each embossed shape just outside the raised area.

3. Arrange the poinsettia pieces in the corners of the layout, with the embossed surfaces face up. This page was made using a commercially available stencil.

▲ POINSETTIAS, SUSAN WALKER, OAKBROOK TERRACE, ILLINOIS

Embossed petals, leaves, and ribbons brighten the festive mood of these Christmas Eve memories. A simple poinsettia motif and bold color scheme create a powerful frame for candid photos of gift-sharing scenes.

▲ CHRISTMAS ABCS, Nancy Wagner, Laguna Beach, California

After losing all her family photos in a house fire, this artist turned to scrapbooking as "a way to tangibly rebuild the past." In these wonderful and whimsical pages, she uses journaling to capture the events and the feeling of Christmas with her family. "Our family together time," she writes, is what makes the day special. She knows that "our memories will last a lifetime—and beyond (if Nancy's scrapbooking does its job)."

◄ DEAR SANTA, Terri Robichon, Plymouth, Minnesota

Children are at the heart of Christmas, and captured moments with Santa make the perfect scrapbook pages. Add a playful touch with primary colors, cut-out crayons, and lettering by whichever youngster has mastered his letters—and you have saved beautiful memories in no time at all!

▼ CHRISTMAS MEMORIES, Donna Pittard, Kingwood, Texas

This festive holiday banner contains lots of journaling about a special Christmas shared by three generations of the Pittard family.

▶ HAPPY NEW
MILLENNIUM 2000,
CHARLA CAMPBELL,
SPRINGFIELD,
MISSOURI

*Where were you when the
new century began? This
scrapbook page records
history for these three children who will someday say,
"I was there."*

▲ WEDDING PORTRAIT, Kristen Mason, Reston, Virginia

This scrapbook title page features a simple frame made of die-cut hearts and doves. Pierced edges add texture to the die cuts. The colors and design of the border convey the mood and style of this couple's special day.

▲ LISA AND DOUGLAS, Pat Murray, Edmonton, Alberta, Canada

Pressed flowers from the bride's bouquet add a special touch to this wedding portrait. Flower stickers extend the theme. Enclose pressed flowers and memorabilia in self-adhesive pockets or slip the page into a page protector.

WEDDINGS AND FORMAL EVENTS

As they do for the big holidays, families also gather together for other types of special events—weddings, christenings, silver or golden anniversaries, for example. These kinds of gatherings are slightly different from holiday gatherings, however. These gatherings have superstars! The couple or the baby at the center of the event is without a doubt the main attraction.

Design your scrapbook pages to reflect that star status. When considering your layout, think about where you will focus attention on the page. Adjust the sizes and placement of images to direct the viewer's eye to the person or people being honored. The portrait of the subject should be the centerpiece of the layout—even if there are photographs of other people on the page, as in the folded-flap wedding page opposite.

Formal occasions usually suggest elegant and sophisticated page designs. Try working with quiet colors and simple motifs, as in the white die-cut heart and dove border shown above left. Add whatever decorative elements best mirror the mood of the event you wish to portray—pressed flowers, memorabilia in protective boxes, silky or lacy fabrics, delicately patterned papers or vellum sheets. Your journaling about the setting, the people, and your own thoughts and feelings will provide an extra layer of meaning. Decorative lettering in special metallic or colored inks add an impressive finishing touch to your page.

▲ WEDDING DOORS, PAM METZGER, BOULDER, COLORADO

Add an extra layer of journaling and photographs to your pages by adding "doors" and "windows" that open.

TRADITIONAL WEDDING ALBUM

In this heirloom scrapbook, the special moments of a couple's wedding day are showcased in a honeycomb pattern. Five rows of hexagons, cut from pastel patterned papers, were adhered to a solid cream background sheet. Some of the hexagons frame photographs cut to the same shape. Five of the patterned "doors" hinge open to reveal more smiles and stories inside!

1. Cut a honeycomb of photographs and printed papers with a hexagon-shaped template. Adhere them to a light-colored, solid sheet. Decide which hexagons you want to open, and carefully cut around five sides of each with a craft knife, using a ruler as a guide. The uncut side will be the "door" hinge.

2. Mount a photograph or a soft plain or patterned paper square on the reverse side of the solid sheet, behind each cut door.

3. Add journaling as desired in the blank areas behind hexagon doors.

> ### TIP
> When using a template to crop photos, move it around on the photo to determine the best position. Lightly mark cutting lines with the small end of an embossing tool.

Chloe
Jan 18, 1998

Winter coat and hat made
with love by Grammy

▲ WEDDING RING, Caroline Lebel, Toronto, Ontario, Canada

Many lovely moments of a spring wedding day are captured on these elegant pages. The candid photographs are integrated into the double-ring quilt pattern and are framed by paper hydrangeas, which are cut to fit the long oval shapes.

◀ CHLOE, Joann Colledge, North Ogden, Utah

Grandmother's gift of a handmade coat and hat are the special treasures featured on Chloe's page. The grapevine that frames Chloe's portrait travels around the page, too, in a border of punched maple leaves and 1/8-inch round shapes.

TIP

When hunting for scrapbooking supplies, be sure to search for papers and fabrics with interesting patterns and textures. Paper doilies, colored tissues, handmade paper, lace napkins, origami papers, crinoline, calico, satins, and velvets— these, and more, add special spark and sparkle to your scrapbook pages.

▲ OUR RINGBEARER, Erin Crawford, San Leandro, California

Erin has always wanted to quilt. Here, she has worked patterned papers and punched-paper hearts, daisies, leaves, and suns into a Dresdan Rose quilt pattern.

◄ MICHAEL'S HOLIDAY, SUSAN COBB FOR HOT OFF THE PRESS

Michael's holiday visit with Grandma is preserved in this delicate page. The photograph is simply tucked into a colored-vellum pocket, which has been layered on a lighter vellum background.

► FRIENDS AND FAMILY, PAM KLASSEN, WESTMINSTER, COLORADO

The French door–style layout makes the most of this page of family photos. The soft and elegant vellum "window panes" create a nostalgic holiday mood.

WORKING WITH VELLUM

Vellum papers add a unique touch to any album page. Because it is transparent, vellum can change the look of solid and patterned papers, but glues, smudges, and creases are also more likely to show. Here are a few simple tricks for working with vellum to create an endless array of special effects.

If you are layering vellum over other papers, choose papers with bright colors and strong patterns so that the colors and patterns will show through. White vellum softens colors or patterns too bold for your page, colored vellum creates additional special effects. Cut vellum only with pattern-edged scissors that have a small pattern. Creases in vellum paper leave white "scars" on the surface.

Ink does not absorb into vellum as quickly as it does into other papers. When journaling on vellum, be sure to let the ink dry for a few minutes before continuing to work with it. For special effects, color on the reverse side of a sheet of vellum with chalk, markers, or colored pencils. The chalk and colored pencils create a soft, muted look; markers will create a stained-glass effect. Because vellum is transparent, it is also perfect for tracing. A "pocket" made of vellum can be a delicate, sheer way to mount a special photo on a page.

Adhesives also don't absorb into the paper as quickly as they do into other types of paper. If you can, work with photo mounts rather than liquid adhesives. Apply all types of adhesives sparingly directly to the matching surface instead of to the vellum. If any glue shows through the vellum sheet, cover the spot with the punched pieces, die cuts, stickers, or drawings.

The Graves

The Calabreze's

Ryan Knutson

Jan Flickinger and grandkids

Seasons Greetings

The Roose's

The Clarks

friends and family for joy

Hailey
Garcia

La Mirada
pumpkin patch
1999

Little
Pumpkin

TOMORROW: TURNING A NEW PAGE

O ne of the greatest gifts that we can give our children is a strong sense of themselves—a sense of who they are, where they came from, and what they hope to become. With this solid self-confidence, they have a better understanding of their place in the world as they make their way through their lives.

Carefully and lovingly made, with an eye toward the future, your family scrapbook will help provide your children with this solid ground. It will also teach them to appreciate and value their ties to their family and heritage. Through your scrapbook, you can share with young family members the long story of your family's shared affection, special achievements, quirks, and fine qualities. The pages of your scrapbook will tell the stories of centuries and trace the smiling faces of generations of loved ones—many of whom often bear a striking resemblance to each other!

Now, add your newcomer's story to the tale. Record the days long before he was a twinkle in your eye and the happy moment when he arrived in the world. Capture her first words, his play time with best friends, her favorite toys, books, and silly expressions. Mix in your own thoughts, hopes, and dreams, and you'll make the pages even more meaningful. Remember, your scrapbook is a personal statement, made with your own hands and creative energy, love, and affection—all of which become part of the gift that you pass along.

◄ LITTLE PUMPKIN, SANDY HOLLY, LAGUNA HILLS, CALIFORNIA

Seasons come and go quickly as children grow. Record memories by combining colors, shapes, and textures that recall special days. Here, cut autumn leaves of vellum from templates of varying sizes are pierced at the edges, and layered to create a feathery effect. The cut out paper pumpkin at bottom right seems to be tumbling out of the photo, adding a bright accent to the page.

▲ LITTLE BLESSINGS STORYBOOK ALBUM, MELISSA MCCALLISTER, GAINESVILLE, FLORIDA

Melissa made four "Little Blessings" books about her daughter, Meghan, as Christmas gifts for Meghan's grandparents and great-grandparents—so they could share the joys of Meghan's first five months of life.

Your family scrapbook will be a source of great joy not only for you, but also for the people you love—a cherished possession that you all turn to again and again. It is a precious heirloom that you will proudly hand down to your children and grandchildren—some who are perhaps still infants, some not yet born. Soon, they will be adding pages and memories of their own—as your family's story continues to unfold through their lifetimes, and beyond.

WELCOME!

When newborns enter our lives, they change everything. After nine months of patient waiting, when time seems to stand still, there is suddenly lots of activity, lots of visitors, and lots of new emotions and discoveries. The pages of your scrapbook will quickly fill with photographs, journaling, and colorful designs that convey the contagious sense of excitement that everyone feels when a new life begins. You'll also want to keep track of baby's first gifts, cards and letters of congratulation, and first experiences—bath time, feedings, and the first smile. The first days and months of a baby's life bustle with rapid growth and miraculous changes. Your scrapbook pages will let you share these thrilling moments with loved ones who live at a distance, but don't want to miss a thing. Design your pages so they retell the story of these extraordinary, fleeting moments—capture the lively playtime activities and the sleepy, quiet moments, too.

▶ SLUMBER SOFTLY LITTLE ONE,
ARTWORK: PAM KLASSEN, WESTMINSTER, COLORADO,
PHOTO: DIANE PERRY, BROOMFIELD, COLORADO

Stamped and heat-embossed stars, sun, and moon fill the skies of this dreamy scene. The sides and lower edges of the cut cloud paper are adhered to the backing, and the top edge is left open as a pocket.

Something for Baby

& Stars

Awaken gently with the sun

& hear the songbirds sing.

3 months

Your baby is the newest link in the chain of your family's deep-rooted and continuing story. Welcome the child by adding his or her own pages to your family album. You will be giving your child a great gift. Your pages will record a significant time in his life that he won't be able to remember. Your pages will also show your child, in years to come, how much she was loved and cared for—and what a central role she played in the family, even then.

◀ SWEET DREAMS, MELISA THORNTON, MUNFORD, TENNESSEE

....

Tender lullabies, splashing baths, first smiles—and even first sniffles and tears. Record all of your growing baby's everyday memories. The years pass quickly, and soon even the simplest, fitful moment will become a precious memory.

▲ INTRODUCING JACK BAYLESS, KATY BAYLESS, ALHAMBRA, CALIFORNIA

....

Katy designed her page announcing the arrival of the newest member of her family around the theme of a growing garden. "Children are like seeds, in each there is a promise of the future," she wrote in her journaling. To add a realistic touch, the lettering resembles the printing on a seed packet.

◀ I THINK THAT I SHALL NEVER SEE, MARYJO REGIER, LITTLETON, COLORADO

....

Old and new photos combine with an old illustration of a ship to link past and present on this page. The portrait at center is the grandfather of these little sailors. His ancestors voyaged from Russia to America in 1879—and more than 100 years later, his four grandsons were born here. This one page tells a century of family history.

▲ GRANDMOTHER'S FLOWER GARDEN, Sally
Swift, Jacksonville, Florida

Sally "stitches" all of her quilts with a black pen. The many variations of patterned paper now available have made creating quilted scrapbook pages more fun, and even more meaningful to avid scrapbookers like Sally.

▲ EMILY, Jennifer Borowski, Princeton,
New Jersey

This simple page shows the many moods of Emily. The paper-pieced bunny at the top of the page is adapted from the design on her outfit. The "stitch" lines are drawn with pen.

LINKS TO THE PAST

Whenever you have the opportunity, scrapbook in words and pictures to record the relationships of your newborn and other family members. Big brothers, little sisters, aunts, and uncles will all play an important part in your newcomer's life. Those relationships begin the day that the baby arrives. Candid photographs of first meetings or touching moments will make beautiful scrapbook pages. Add some journaling, too—gift-card poems or messages, stories or bits of information about the life of the adult relative. Include a few of your own hopes and dreams for your baby's future, too.

Records of the first meetings or special bonds between grandparents (or great-grandparents!) and the newborn are important documents, full of emotion and special value. As the older members of your family age, recording the times you share becomes more and more important. A new baby in the family certainly gives you the chance to scrapbook about a meaningful and happy event. More important, it gives you the chance to scrapbook about the great and rare opportunity that these generations—sometimes separated in time by almost a hundred years—have to meet and know each other.

Your child has been born into a personal universe that is filled with stories, traditions, and lots of love. Your child's story stretches back in time, just as, with this new life, your family's story now continues to move forward into the future. Your scrapbook pages can be the bridge.

EMILY'S HEIRLOOM QUILT

Six months before Emily Rose Stevenson was born, her grandmother, Marjorie Mann, and her aunt, Janet van Trueren, began making her a very special quilt. The quilt combined old and new fabrics, including pieces from the baby's great-great-grandmother, pearl beads from her mother's bridal veil, and swatches from her mother's childhood clothing. The quilt was presented to Emily on her first birthday and hangs on her bedroom wall. Emily's mother, Tammy, added these pages to Emily's scrapbook to remind her daughter how much she is dearly loved. She photographed each of the quilt blocks and "pieced" them with paper pieces. Her journaling page tells the story of this beautiful gift.

—*Tammy Stevenson, Florissant, Missouri*

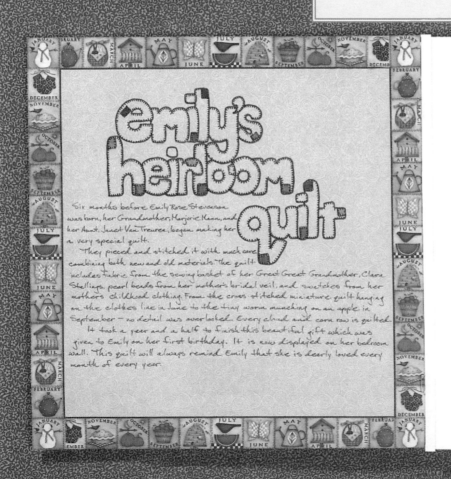

▲ HUG ME 1ST, 2ND, 3RD AND 4TH!, LINDA STRAUSS, PROVO, UTAH, PHOTOS: TRICIA KELLY, THOUSAND OAKS, CALIFORNIA

Stamped babies and tiny ribbons are tucked in the memorabilia holder— placeholders for future locks of hair from each of the four Kelly quadruplets.

▶ IT'S THE LITTLE THINGS, WENDY MCKEEHAN FOR PUZZLEMATES

This delicately patterned album cover announces the stars of the pages inside this lovely scrapbook. Photographs and journaling of everyday life will tell the story of Mommy and Tori as they get to know each other.

It's The Little Things

Mommy & Tori 1999

   Children are the heart of the family

 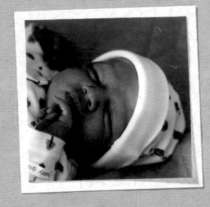  

   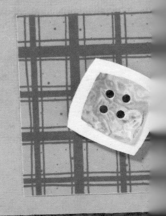

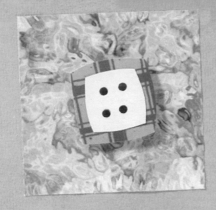

Mommy
Daddy
and
Sawyer
1998

What says it better than these patchwork-style pages? Layers of patterned-paper scraps and punched paper, foam-mounted "buttons" alternate with simple snapshots of Mommy, Daddy, and Sawyer.

Each year as the family gathers to exchange gifts, we place lighted candles in the windows. This tradition goes back to great-grandma's family. Before Jodie would open her first present this year, she had to light the candles. Great-grandma would be so happy. December 24, 2000

▲ AUSTEN AND MOMMY, Cindy Mandernach, Grand Blanc, Michigan

The mix of black-and-white and color photographs captures the timelessness of mother's love. The photos were cropped with a variety of decorative scissors.

◄ VELLUM CANDLES, Pam Klassen, Westminster, Colorado

Just as their great-grandmother always did, each Christmas holiday, this family lights candles in the windows as they gather to exchange their gifts. The layered vellum creates the perfect luminescent effect of candlelight. Vellum is also perfect for snow, stars, clouds, smoke, and sunshine.

MAKING NEW MEMORIES

Don't stop scrapbooking when they take their first steps! As your baby grows and changes—into a toddler, then a youngster, then a kid, then teenager—there will be plenty more to scrapbook about. Your child will have many new experiences and forge many new relationships, both with family and with friends. The favorite toys, the first days of school, the best pals, the Cub Scout outings—all of these are a part of your child's life story. Each deserves to be recorded and preserved on special pages of their own.

The Baby Boy who Could

AT SIX MONTHS

I want Ben's toys (especially his little cars)... I can take off my shoes and socks in about two seconds with a great big grin and have lost them everywhere (HEB, the street, etc.)... I love to ride in the front of the stroller and flirt with the ladies at the mall... I'm really cute!

AT FOUR MONTHS

I can work my way over to my "two headed bird" toy and pull it off the Gymini... I'm always losing my left sock... I have two teeth on the bottom... I love to laugh at Ben when he says "great big hug"...

NOAH'S ARK

A · YEAR · IN · S.S. NOAH & CO.

NOAH

Noah's 2nd Year Highlights
1998-1999

Birthday Party Theme: Dragon
Soda of Choice: "Dr. Rootbeer"
Rite of Passage: Ditched the Diapers, Rides a Trike
Meanest Idea: Cutting Up Brothers Pokemon Card
Bestest Playmate: "My Friend" (pretend pal)
Game: "Who wants to play, baby bird raise their hand?"
Bad Game: Does That Hurt?
T. V: 7:30am Zoboomafoo
Best Name Drop: "Jesus told me I sleep with You!"
Stern Quote: "You see that sign, That sign says
                 NO _____!" (fill in blank with Noah's agenda)
Likely to Note Seat Belt Violations & Profanity:
Song Written: "I'm working on It's My Happy Day"
Bad Habits: Blowfish Marathons & Loud Burping
Noah's Lang: Add a "Y" to the end of words
Most Sensitive to Temperature: "Coldy!"
Noah's Profanity: "You Hockey Pockey!"
Most Embarrassing Dad Moment: Pulling Down Dads
                 Pants to Show People his "Boo Boo"
Quote to Stranger: "My Mom Pees Out of her Bottom!"
Oddest Bedtime Ritual: Kicking Himself to Sleep
Best & Worst Attribute: Easily Delighted & Offended
Best Show: Jets Taking Off After Air Show!
Goals for Next Year: Ride a Trolley, Scare My Brother,
                 Dress Myself, Jump Into the Pool
Halloween Costume: Telletubbie
Occupational Goal: "Be A Ghost"
Favorite Sport: Anything in Water!
Best Habit: Holding Hands

▲ THE BABY BOY WHO COULD, *(previous spread)* JENNIFER BROOKOVER, SAN ANTONIO, TEXAS

Little boys love trains, and this little climber takes Jennifer's baby boy on his first six-month journey. Silhouetted and cropped photos of her passenger travel in a train of primary-colored die cuts on a track of small brown rectangles layered on a thin black line. The mountains are photos pieced together and cut along their top edge. Puffy light-blue cut clouds tell the story with letter stickers and hand journaling.

◀ NOAH'S ARK, SUSAN BADGETT, NORTH HILLS, CALIFORNIA

A classic Bible story is the theme for these pages featuring Noah's birthday celebration and highlights of his past year. Susan decided to simplify her life by creating a two-page layout for each child each year—a very "can-do" project.

VELVET STAMPING

Velvet paper stamped with decorative motifs adds elegance to scrapbook pages and album covers. Be sure to work with acid-free velvet paper. You'll also need an iron warmed to a medium setting, stamps with simple motifs, and a teflon pressing cloth or paper bag.

1. Place the stamp on the ironing board, rubber side up. Cut the teflon pressing cloth or paper bag to the size of the velvet paper. This sheet will protect the velvet from the heat and imprint of the iron.

2. Place the velvet paper, right side down, onto the stamp. Be sure that the stamp is positioned so that the design motif will be exactly where you want it. Lay the pressing cloth or paper bag on top of the velvet. Press the iron onto the pressing sheet for about 30 seconds. Do not move the iron while pressing. Now, lift the sheets away from the stamp. The velvet paper will have a reverse-embossed image.

3. If you would like to add color, simply apply ink to your stamp before ironing the image onto your paper. If you choose to use velvet fabric instead of velvet paper, simply mist both sides of the velvet with water before ironing.

TIP

*B*e sure to include an assortment of rubber stamps in your stash of scrapbooking supplies. They are available in various sizes, shapes, and patterns—including alphabet stamps, border stamps, and theme stamps. Ink pads in a variety of colors will make stamped designs jump right off the page.

◄ NICOLE AND ISABEL,
ARTWORK: ERIKIA GHUMM,
BRIGHTON, COLORADO, PHOTO:
OREALYS HERNANDEZ, HOLLY
SPRINGS, NORTH CAROLINA

Muted colors and the soft elegance of velvet beg to be touched. The "reverse embossed" flowers created with simple rubber stamps and a warm iron provide the ultimate decorative touch. Just try not to run your hand across the page!

LOVE AT FIRST SIGHT, TINA BURTON, MOUNDS, OKLAHOMA

Carey will be able to remember Dodger's first litter of kittens—and how he just couldn't put them down, no matter what—just by looking at this adorable page. Colorful mats and small punched circles and mini hearts frame two simply cropped photos, while the whole cut-out crew snuggling in a cheery wagon is silhouetted against a plain white background. The polka dot blanket is edged with decorative scissors and a mouse adhered to the sign enjoys the view.

◄ "I LOVE BOOKS," MISSY RICE, WHITTIER, CALIFORNIA

Missy completed these pages about her son's love of books before he was diagnosed as high-functioning autistic. "That makes the page all the more special," she says. Missy has included titles and paper illustrations of several of Zachary's favorite books, along with photographs of friends and family reading to him.

FINGERPRINT ART

Kids can add a special signature mark to scrapbook pages—their fingerprints! Select several colors of stamping ink. Stamp thumbprints and fingerprints around the edges of the scrapbook page. Press firmly and lift carefully to avoid smearing the prints. Use colored pens to transform the prints into animal figures or other designs.

▲ THUMBPRINTS, BEVERLEE BOND, GARDEN GROVE, CALIFORNIA

As her birthday gift, Beverlee's children stamped and drew these cute little creatures for her scrapbook page, starting first with their own thumbprints.

▶ MICE IN THE CUPBOARDS, CHARLA CAMPBELL, SPRINGFIELD, MISSOURI

The pantry was the source for props for this clever layout. Charla took pictures of costumed children in various sitting, standing, or crawling positions. The photos of the pantry items are sized to fit right in with the children's antics. Silhouetted against a black background, the photos are positioned on tan strips to represent shelves. Journaling with a silver pen completes the page.

No! There's mice in the cupboards..... squeak.

stamper..... squeak..... Madison.....Brittany.....Kayla.....Tyler.....

▲ LET IT SNOW, Amy Eshelman, Indianapolis, Indiana

Fourteen-year-old Amy believes it is important to capture the memories of her youth. A combination of die-cut snowflakes, simple shaped, cropped, matted photos, and silhouetted photos tumble across the inventively journaled snow drifts in fun-loving profusion.

◄ BEST BUDDIES, Cathie Allan, Edmonton, Alberta, Canada

Would that we could all see these fabulous "best buddies" in ten or fifteen years!

AS CHILDREN GROW

Add pages for each of your children as they grow, and, when they are old enough, encourage them to make their own pages, too. Even little kids can add their rainbow-colored handprints or crooked crayon lettering to the pages you are designing about their special achievements or favorite foods. Junior scrapbookers like fourteen-year-old Amy Eshelman became so excited about her mother's scrapbooking project that she decided to start a scrapbook of her own. Now, she and her mother attend crop parties together every Friday night, and Amy has even introduced scrapbooking to her friends.

A family's story is truly never-ending. Each generation has its own tale to tell. Your scrapbooks—and your children's and your grandchildren's scrapbooks—will link those tales together in a beautiful, imaginative, and wholly individual way.

No one can tell your family's story better than you.

TEMPLATES

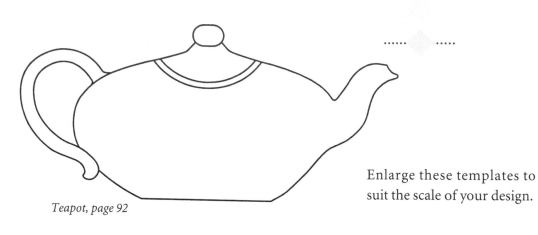

Teapot, page 92

..... ◆ .....

Enlarge these templates to
suit the scale of your design.

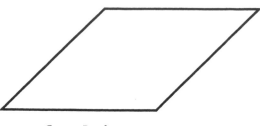

Cevron Patch, page 36

Pop-up, pages 82-83

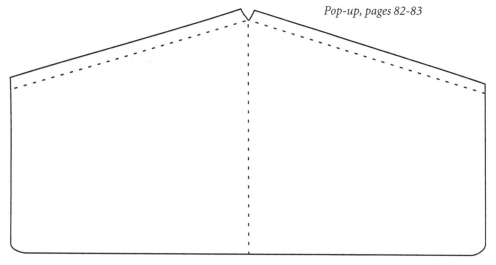

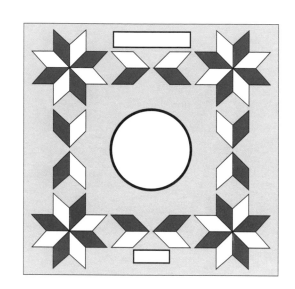

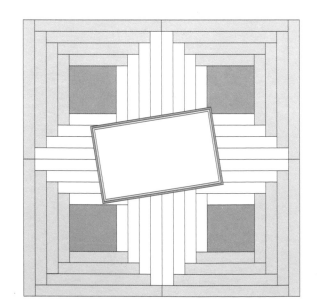

Illusion Pattern, page 69

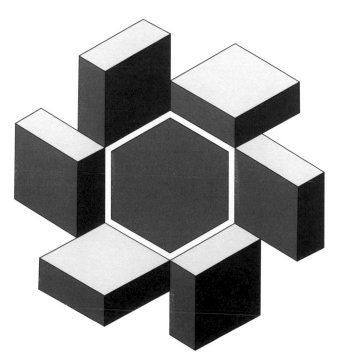

Log Cabin, pages 39

SOURCE GUIDE

SOURCE GUIDE COMPANY LISTINGS

Accu-Cut® (800) 288-1670
All My Memories (888) 553-1998
American Traditional™ Stencils (800) 278-3624
Art Gone Wild! (800) 945-3980
Art Impressions (800)393-2014
Artful Additions fishscraps@uswest.net
Artistic Wire Ltd.™ (630) 530-7567
Back Street, Inc. (678) 206-7373
Canson (800) 628-9283
Carl Mfg. USA, Inc. (800) 257-4771
Carolee's Creations™ (435) 563-1100
    wholesale only
Clearsnap Inc. (800) 448-4862
Close To My Heart (888) 655-6552
Cock-A-Doodle Design, Inc. (800) 262-9727
Colorbök (800) 366-4660 wholesale only
Colors By Design (800) 832-8436
Creative Beginnings (800) 367-1739
Creative Imaginations (800) 942-6487
Creative Memories® (800) 468-9335
Current®, Inc. (800) 848-2848
Cut-It-Up™ (530) 389-2233
D. J. Inkers™ 800-325-4890
Dayco Ltd. 877-595-8160
Delta Technical Coatings, Inc. 800-423-4135
Design Originals 800-877-7820
Dover Publications 800-223-3130
Ellis on® Craft & Design 800-253-2238
Emagination Crafts Inc. 630-833-9521
Family Treasures, Inc. 800-413-2645
Fiskars, Inc. 800-950-0203
Frances Meyer, Inc.® 800-372-6237
Geographics, Inc. 800-426-5923
Gina Bear, Ltd. 888-888-4453
Hallmark Cards, Inc. 800-425-6275
Handmade Scraps, Inc. 877-915-1695
Hero Arts Rubber Stamps, Inc. 800-822-4376
Holly Craft 949-583-1426
Hot Off The Press 800-227-9595
Hot Potatoes 615-269-8002
Hygloss Products, Inc. 201-458-1700
JD Impressions 559-276-1633
Judi-Kins 310-515-1115
K & Company 816-389-4150

Kangaroo & Joey®, Inc. 800-646-8065
Keeping Memories Alive™ 800-419-4949
Lake City Craft Co. 417-725-8444
Making Memories 800-286-5263 wholesale only
Microsoft Corp. www.microsoft.com
MiniGraphics 800-442-7035
Mrs. Grossman's Paper Co. 800-457-4570
Nag Posh™ 800-333-3279
Northern Spy 530-620-7430
NRN Designs 800-421-6958 wholesale only
Paper Adventures® 800-727-0699
Papers By Catherine 713-723-3334
Pebbles In My Pocket® pebbles@pebblesin
    mypocket.com
Plaid Enterprises, Inc. 800-842-4197
Posh Impressions 800-421-7674
Pressed Petals, Inc. 800-748-4656
PrintWorks 800-854-6558 wholesale only
Provo Craft® 888-577-3545
PSX Design 800-782-6748
Puzzle Mates™ 888-595-2887
Rospak, Inc. PO Box 266 Armonk, NY 10504
Royal Stationery™ / Masterpiece® Studios
    800-447-0219
Rubber Stampede 800-423-4135
Rubber Stamps of America 800-553-5031
S.R.M. Press Inc. 800-323-9589
Sandylion Sticker Designs 800-387-4215
Sonburn, Inc. 800-527-7505
SpotPen, Inc. 505-523-8820
Stampabilities 800-888-0321
Stampendous!®/Mark Enterprises 800-869-0474
Stampin' Up! 800-782-6787
Stamping Station Inc. 801-444-3828
Stickopotamus® 888-270-4443
Susan A. Designs 978-458-6700 wholesale only
The C-Thru® Ruler Company 800-243-8419
The Crafter's Workshop 877-CRAFTER
The Family Archives™ 888-622-6556
    wholesale only
The Marshall Company Brandess-Kalt-Aetna
    Group, Inc. 800-621-5488
The Paper Catalog (FLAX San Francisco)
    888-727-3763
The Paper Company 800-426-8989
The Paper Patch® 800-397-2737 wholesale only
The Robin's Nest 435-789-5387
The Uptown Design Company 253-925-1234
Westrim Crafts/Memories Forever®
    800-727-2727
Wübie Prints 888-256-0107 wholesale only

ILLUSTRATED GLOSSARY OF TECHNIQUES

COLLAGE

Collage is a collection of different photographs or other images pasted together on a page. The elements may or may not overlapage See page 70.

CROPPING

Cropping means trimming away outside edges of your photos. Cropping is used to get rid of unwanted or unnecessary parts of the photo or to make the photo fit a particular size and shape of space. See page 26.

DIE-CUT FRAMES

Die-cut frames are commercially available in a variety of designs and sizes. They can be adapted to suit your own needs by additional cutting or mounting. See page 54.

EMBOSSING

Embossing involves making a paper design three-dimensional by rubbing it on a raised surface with an embossing stylus, or you can create an embossed image with embossing powder and a heat source (heat gun). See pages 115-116.

FINGERPRINT ART

Finger- and thumbprints can be used as stamps to create a special signature scrapbook page. Decorated with colored pens the prints become handmade animal figures or other designs. See page 135.

JOURNALING

Journaling is just what its name implies, writing the story of your pages in words. Journaling can be as simple as a name and/or date, or it can be a full essay of the event commemorated on your page. It can also be lyrics from a favorite song, or a poem that has special meaning for you. See pages 10-13.

LIFT-THE-FLAPS

Lift-the-flaps pages have windows of paper that you open to reveal a photo or journaling surprise. See page 109.

MATTING

Matting is putting a frame of paper around your photo. You can place the photo onto a piece of paper that is the same shape but slightly larger than the image or make a cutout frame and placing your photograph behind it See page 28.

MONTAGE

Montage is similar to collage, but the pictures or parts of pictures are superimposed, or overlapped, so that they form a blended whole. See page 22.

MOSAIC

Mosaic is basically the same for the scrapbook artist as the tile artist. You cut photos into small shapes and place them on a page separated by space or a line. Photos could be cut into uniform squares and placed on a page with uniform space around each element. See page 7.

MOUNTING

Mounting simply means applying your photos or other art to your scrapbook page. See page 36.

POP-UP

Pop-up is the art of cutting, folding and mounting so that when you open a two-page spread a design will "pop up" from the pages. See page 82.

PAPER FOLDING

Paper folding is the art of folding paper to create designs. It involves techniques similar to origami and kirigami to produce frames, borders, and embellishments for a scrapbook page. See page 20.

PUNCH ART

Punch art uses any kind of paper punched into a shape with any of the many punches made especially for this purpose. The punched-out shapes may be used as they are or folded and combined with other shapes to create a new image. See page 74.

PAPER LAYERING

Paper layering can mean cutting out parts of a design to allow a different colored paper to show through, or placing light paper, like vellum, over an image to screen or soften the image or color underneath.. See page 112.

QUILLING

Quilling is a simple decorative technique used to embellish any kind of page. Simply roll thin strips of paper around a slotted or needle tool into various shapes and then arrange and combine the shapes to create your own design. See page 51.

PAPER PIECING

Paper piecing is a technique used to construct a cut paper image from various sources—punches, free-hand shapes, or template designs. See page 114.

SINGLE-FOLD CUTTING

Single-fold paper cutting lets you create a perfectly symmetrical design. Fold a piece of scrap paper in half, sketch one half of the design and cut it out. When you unfold the paper, you have a symmetrical template to use on your "real" paper. See page 75.

PAPER QUILTING

Quilt patterns lend themselves beautifully to scrapbooking pages; the logic and format make them irresistible. Quilt designs, cut from various shaped patterns, are adapted to create stunning borders, frames, or even the central motif on a large page. See page 76.

TEMPLATES

Templates are patterns used as guides in creating a drawn or cut image. See page 19.